GARDENS FOR THE 21ST CENTURY

GARDENS
FOR THE 21ST CENTURY
ANITA PEREIRE

AURUM PRESS

First published in Great Britain 1999 by Aurum Press Ltd
25 Bedford Avenue, London WC1B 3AT

This paperback edition first published in 2001 by Aurum Press
Copyright © Anita Pereire 1999, 2001

A catalogue record for this book is available from the British Library.

ISBN 1 85410 799 2

Edited and project managed by Judy Spours
Designed by David Fordham

Typeset by MATS, Southend-on-Sea, Essex
Originated by Colorlito-CST, Milan
Printed in Italy by Artegrafica S.p.A, Verona

Frontispiece A tiered, pyramid effect closes a vista in Charles Jencks' garden.

Page 1 Cosmology is the inspiration for Charles Jencks' garden in the Scottish Borders, hence this inscription - the world 'relativity' can be read, from whichever side you look.

Title page Sheets of coloured glass and mirrors create a colourful roof-garden scene by Martha Schwartz.

CONTENTS

Introduction   9

C O N T E N T S

The spectacular tree fern *Dicksonia antarctica* has grown at Heligan in Cornwall, England since the nineteenth century.

Hydrangeas are an important element of the planting schemes at Vasterival near Dieppe, France. This deep blue variety is called 'Vicomtesse de Vibraye'.

INTRODUCTION

Left The 'foot' maze at Conholt Park, Hampshire, England. *Above* 'Sea Change' sculpture by George Cutts in Hat Hill Copse, Sussex, England.

MY AIM IN WRITING THIS BOOK has been to gather together and illustrate outstanding examples of what is new, interesting and likely to stand the test of time in gardening and garden design as the old century gives way to the new. Unavoidably, the gardens are a personal choice, although I have tried to respect the views of leading gardeners in the five continents discussed in the book when making my selection.

The gardens I have presented here are the work of many talented people. Some are controversial in their approach, setting out to astonish or even unsettle the visitors to their gardens. On the other hand, some gardens, such as the beautiful creation of Princess Sturdza in France or Caroline Tisdall's garden at Conholt in southern England, are included not because they represent a new style of gardening, but rather a new commitment to ecological principles.

I have included the original work of Martha Schwartz because it epitomizes American vigour and daring, and the

work of the Popes at Hadspen House in England as a wonderful example of what an educated eye can bring to the creation of a herbaceous border. Their work illustrates the increasing trend for people trained in the fine or decorative arts to display their talents in the garden.

The unique work of Charles Jencks in Scotland is here because there is nothing like it anywhere in the world. Jencks bases his landscaping on the principles inherent in post-Einsteinian physics, but the observer does not need to understand its complexities in order to be stunned and enchanted by the results. The Casses' sculpture gardens at Hat Hill Copse in southern England exemplify the marked increase in the imaginative placing of outdoor sculpture, while Keir Davidson's transformation of a stretch of countryside in New York State shows how the manipulation of quarried stone and water systems is increasingly used to transform entire landscapes.

The garden which spans both the indoors and the outdoors is another important trend. Extending the house by means of a patio or terrace where the family can gather, and where the plants are mainly container grown, is becoming popular worldwide. Countries with warm climates have had patios for centuries; now, with the proliferation of potted plants that can be protected during the winter season, the patio has become a possibility in many geographical areas. Plants from all over the world, grown and distributed in containers, are arriving on the foreign markets, making an African, Mexican or Caribbean patio show accessible. As a result, the concept of a 'garden room' is now widely recognized.

I detect a marked *fin-de-siècle* nostalgia, most evident in Britain in the revised interest in the old arts of creating mazes and grottoes, and by Tim Smit's restoration of the garden at Heligan in Cornwall. In France, it is at its best in the outstanding example of revived medievalism at the Abbaye d'Orsan. Water is increasingly an important element of garden design, whether a modest tub in a small garden or an ambitious lake in a large landscape. New materials and techniques have made water features affordable and easy to manage.

I believe we should also take note also of work influenced by the contemporary fine arts, often exploiting the implantation of 'found' objects and bric-à-brac of various kinds into the garden, where it masquerades as sculpture. This is to be seen in Ian Hamilton Finlay's Scottish garden and at Daniel Spoerri's 'Il Giardino' in Italy, both of which weave a greater meaning amongst the plants. Some of the work is controversial, as indeed it is meant to be, and it will doubtless influence a number of young designers creating the gardens of the new century.

I have touched only briefly on the genetic engineering of plants, since it is still in its infancy, so far applied mainly in Australia and Japan for the cut-flower trade. But, surely, the experts will be offering us that elusive blue rose for our gardens before long. The fact that I can personally do very well without it is neither here nor there.

Over-arching all these trends and innovations is the spectre of climate change, which will have a fundamental impact on our gardens as the new century progresses. It appears that the temperate zones will become distinctly less so, with temperature swings and rainfall and wind

Below A gentleman waits for afternoon tea amongst the hellebores in the secret garden at Conholt Park, Hampshire, England.

Right In the Majorelle garden in Marrakesh, Morocco, stately palm trees tower above a pergola and other formal elements of the garden

A large bronze fountain sculpted by Otto Fried sprays delicate jets of water into a stream that runs through a private garden in France.

characteristics which we can as yet only dimly perceive. Will we be growing Mediterranean flowers in Scotland and bog plants in the South of France? What will increased wind velocities do to our choice of trees? And what of the lack of frosts in winter? Certainly, as global warming allows us to plant and maintain many more warm climate plants, 'dry' gravel gardens are very much in demand, possessing the additional advantages of being easy to plant and to maintain. Gardening is likely to be very different when the new century ends in its turn.

Today, gardening has become the most popular leisure activity – art, hobby or whatever you want to call or make of it – in the development of which the media is playing an important, democratizing role. One of the most widely established facts is that more and more people are gardening themselves on a substantial scale, whereas in the past they employed outside labour. Gardeners are an insatiable group, always seeking rare plants and fresh ideas, and from the further afield the better. Without turning our backs on the most beautiful gardens conceived during the twentieth century, we have to admit that gardening cannot stand still. We are not sweeping under the compost heap the legacy of Jekyll, Sackville-West or Lloyd, any more than the twentieth century ignored such eminent predecessors as William Kent, Le Notre and Capability Brown. But there's more to come: exciting new options, valid essential revivals, new garden design talents – and I have enjoyed introducing you to some of them.

GOING ORGANIC

Beyond doubt, the most important development in gardening that the new century inherits from the old is a worldwide move towards organic principles. This basic shift in our attitude towards the natural environment is new. It represents a realization that we simply cannot continue to treat our ecosystem with contempt, dosing it daily with chemicals promoted by corporations which understand the value of a profit margin, but not that of a bee, a butterfly or a frog. We have realized that the wonderful variety of plant species is there to be enjoyed, and therefore treasured and preserved, and that we are privileged tenants among many others on our planet, not its sole owners.

Even though our ideas about gardening and its relationship to the environment may be changing, there is still a long row to hoe before gardening organically ceases to be a minority interest and becomes, once again, the norm. We do not need to be compost fanatics or butterfly worshippers to adopt such a course – just true lovers of nature, gently modified and nurtured by humankind.

The valley at Vasterival winds through lush osmunda ferns that thread their way along a woodland stream. The scene is lit up by groups of the white, fragrant flowering zantedeschia that emerge from under the overhanging trees along the bank.

The 'secret garden' at Conolt Park is enclosed by tall yew hedges and *Helleborus orientalis*, which, together with artichokes and topiarized balls of box, creates a green harmony from which spring bulbs will appear.

ORGANICS FOR ALL SEASONS

◆

CONHOLT PARK HAMPSHIRE, ENGLAND

CAROLINE TISDALL

The circular garden surrounding the fountain is seasonal. Here it is dressed for one of its summer shows with a ground cover of *Alchemilla mollis* dotted with verbascum.

To DESCRIBE THE GARDEN at Conholt as lavish would be an understatement. All the traditional garden components are here, but are used in an untraditional manner.

Caroline Tisdall, writer, poet, photographer and film-maker, designed and gardens it herself. Her background as an art historian is clear in her sense of form in design, while her commitment to the countryside as a leading conservationist dictates her organic approach to gardening.

Conholt has an ecological vocation. Manure of every sort is the garden's foundation, for the soil is only an inch or two deep over pure chalk. Lordy, the Shire horse who pulls the game-cart in winter, provides the bulk of the manure, which, with more from pigs, wild boar, bison and chickens, plus home-made compost, replaces chemicals and fertilizers. Ladybirds and lacewings, scratching chickens and pheasants, partridge and slug-eating ducks keep the bugs at bay, as do generous interplantings of herbs. Confronted with a two-acre, empty (since the War), walled kitchen garden with a broken down wall, Caroline chose first to create a water centrepiece in front of the restored Edwardian conservatory. She then composed a planting scheme which rolls through the seasons: one for early spring of white daffodils and perfumed narcissi; one for late spring of white tulips to flower over a two-month period; and one for summer and into autumn of courgettes planted into a blanket of manure, with lush late irises and *Alchemilla mollis*, given height by the yellow candles of self-sown verbascum.

The secret garden initiates its spring flowering with a heavily perfumed path edging of hyacinths and more discreet aconitums. The planting is given a neat formality by the box balls at the corners of the beds.

Either side of this central pond are two radiating 'cartwheels', one edged with box for a vegetable and fruit potager, the other with lavender for a flower garden. She favours organic, exotic vegetables such as asparagus, peas, black beans and whole collections of different sorts of rhubarb, potatoes and berries. There are flamboyant plantings of artichokes and cardoons underplanted with red *Atriplex hortensis* 'Rubra', a glorious colour contrast, and opium poppies are encouraged to self-seed among the vegetables.

At the centre of the cartwheels are rose and honeysuckle arbours, from which gravel paths radiate, cleverly concealed as they wind their way into the densely planted areas of the flower garden. Here, lavender hedges jostle more artichokes, whose architectural grey foliage and brilliant violet flowers join in a year-round firework display of blue, purple, grey and white.

Osmanthus, tulips and hellebores give way to a huge collection of alliums and hardy geraniums, above which tower tree peonies and choisya. Then standard peonies jostle with ceanothus, delphiniums, irises and nepeta, giving way to agapanthus, perovskia, buddleia, stunning banks of *Hydrangea arborescens* 'Annabelle', and sweet-smelling carpets of marjoram for the bees. This is no classical herbaceous or vegetable border arrangement, but generous groupings of plants which come into their own one after another. Neither is this a low-maintenance garden, but rather one created to promote planting ideas and to feed large numbers of people.

All possible planting opportunities are taken. Walls — of which there are plenty, with outhouses, stables, workshops — are all dressed with climbers, such as ceanothus, clematis, fruit trees, roses, honeysuckle and wisteria. Throughout the garden, associations between plants are daring and inventive, but not contrived: pink nerines with lavender for autumn; blue agapanthus and lavender or white lilies for summer; and self-seeding poppies. . . when they feel like it.

In its little home-made, organic basket of chicken wire lined with a duvet of straw, rhubarb can be kept warm for the winter.

In a protected corner of what was – and still partly is – the vegetable garden, fig trees thrive against the warm brick wall and *Hydrangea arborescens* 'Annabelle' make a spectacular display during the summer months.

Three-metre tall hedges of over-grown yews – quite possibly two hundred years old – have been reclaimed and fed. They now embrace a secret garden of green sloping banks – once the natural cesspit of the old house – opportunistically planted with moisture-loving hostas, bulbs and hellebores. It is within this inner sanctuary that Caroline chose to erect a small garden library-retreat, tucked away where a sense of calm and privacy prevails.

A mysterious, winding, hedged-in path made of slices of a huge old beech tree that fell in a storm leads to a bee garden, where the hives have been cleverly integrated into a

Caroline has created an unusual herb feature in the Shakespeare garden with an oyster-shell frame surrounding potted parsley. It is encircled with sprigs of euonymus and perfumed rosemary.

nectar-haven of white wisteria clambering up oak columns decked with vines of black grapes. The bee house itself was converted from an old apple store in the local style and reminds us that bees are a vital part of the pollination process in gardening, fruit growing and agriculture. They are threatened by disease, chemicals and genetically modified crops, and Conholt is their haven.

The bee garden leads down to a rose garden. Caroline's preference is for old roses, those with long flowering seasons and strong perfumes. Three rings of box-edged circles within an oblong are surrounded by bold swags of Rosa 'Mme Alfred Carrière' on ropes. In the outer ring are tough and rewarding Rugosas.

Caroline and her partner Paul are currently creating a laurel maze on a long plot in the garden. It is shaped like a huge right foot, complete with long, painted toenails. Its paths are three metres wide, mulched with ecologically-sound bark chippings, and the toenails are planted with self-sowing red atriplex to achieve the desired effect. The foot motif adapts well to its long, thin site and its toes give the opportunity for five additional, mini-mazes. The foot also implies the idea of a journey or a pilgrimage and, best of all, it is fun to see friends get lost inside a giant foot!

A temple of Indian inspiration is dressed with *Solanum jasminoides* 'Album', winter jasmine and the rose 'Alberic Barbier'. Beds are planted with chimonanthus, hamamelis and the rose 'Anita Pereire'.

WILD FLOWERS RETURN

◆

ASHTON WOLD, PETERBOROUGH, ENGLAND

MIRIAM ROTHSCHILD

IN THE MIDDLE AGES, the summer meadows of Europe were ablaze with wild flowers. Only half a century ago, the ridges and furrows of our hayfields were still lacquered with buttercups and perfumed by the scent of cowslips. But in the late twentieth century, equipped with powerful machinery and potent chemicals, we have flattened the ridges, drained the soil and eliminated the flowering 'idle weeds', leaving only economically viable mono-crops of well-fertilized grasses.

Miriam Rothschild, a biologist but above all a dedicated naturalist, describes how she awoke one morning in the 1960s, gazed out at the distant uniform green fields visible from her window in Ashton Wold, near Peterborough, and exclaimed in dismay: 'A snooker table! I'm living on a snooker table!' At that moment she was inspired to start out on her first wild plant experiment, that of restoring a flowering hayfield on the lawn in front of her house.

It took Miriam Rothschild years of trial seeding in small areas to achieve this wild flower field. So natural, so beautiful, so easy, to all appearances, but a feat which requires careful annual supervision to prevent grass from taking over.

The actual making of a flowering hayfield was really hard work. She had to combine serious scientific principles with aesthetic charm and simultaneously conserve both rare and common species of plants. Furthermore, she had to create and then oversee an environment which would last for many years. There were few clues to guide her in her task, as very little is known about the deliberate cultivation of wild flowers. One very delightful surprise was in store for her. Despite some seventy years of persistent, regular and careful mowing, once the lawn was left alone and allowed to grow naturally, many broad-leaved flowering plants suddenly appeared. There were daisies, buttercups, hawkweed, the odd cowslip, dandelions, speedwell, bird's-foot trefoil, clover, hoary plantain, stitchwort, lady's bedstraw, eyebright, fairy flax, quaking grass, brilliant self-heal and even bee orchids!

Nearby her garden were several deserted wartime airfields where a fair variety of wild flowers flourished and could be collected. Miriam selected quite a few species which had

A corner of a summer-flowering meadow of cornflowers, marigolds and ox-eye daisies. The flowers start in May and continue through to July.

A daisy field that can flourish in all kinds of grassland, flowering from May until September, is pictured here in full bloom. The proper name of the species is *Leucanthemum vulgare*.

Although this looks like a hand-planted garden, this strikingly patterned, drooping, tulip-shaped bulb is the rare *Fritillaria meleagris*. It sometimes escapes from the garden to colonize in meadows, where it is a bumble bee's delight.

not appeared spontaneously in the uncut lawn, or only rarely, such as restharrow, sainfoin and cowslips, and she planted them on patches of her hayfield which she scraped bare of soil. From there they spread slowly across the field, in wider and wider circles, so that in the twentieth year after their original transplantation the local botanical society counted ten thousand cowslip plants in flower. Altogether, ninety different species of broad-leaved plants and grasses were eventually identified growing in the mini-hayfield. The penny dropped: the secret was the absence of chemicals. Miriam became a pioneer of the cultivation and conservation of the wild flowers and grasses of the United Kingdom.

Next she tackled a large kitchen garden. One half of the available space was planted with rows of radishes, lettuce and the like, with primroses, oxlip, field geraniums, heartsease, chicory and other such wild plants colonizing the remaining areas. The soil was well weeded, lightly limed, well dug and raked. In the other half of the garden, she grew wild flowers in trial beds in order to find the most appealing combinations for borders and beds, window boxes and odd bare corners. Perhaps the most attractive mixture, and one easy to grow, was christened 'Farmer's Nightmare'. It consisted of poppies, cornflowers, corn marigolds, corn cockles, daisies, feverfew and, in fact, all the well-known weeds of arable crops, past and present. A sprinkling of wild oats and barley was added.

Finally, Miriam Rothschild transformed the entire, conventional Edwardian garden of her Ashton Wold home. In the past, it had been well supplied with fruit trees, laburnum, white and mauve lilacs and philadelphus. These had neither been trimmed or pruned and had grown into surprisingly tall trees, reaching for the light above a variety of flowering bushes. Miriam planted wild cherry trees alongside the stone steps and in groups beside the terrace walls. Crab apples and pear trees were added, with honeysuckle climbing up into the branches. The centre of the courtyard was planted with copper-leaved prunus, Judas trees, and beneath them, spring-flowering bulbs. Except for a circular gravel path round the courtyard and another along the front of the house, the rest of the garden was grassed over and left uncut; wild flowers were encouraged to grow everywhere.

Miriam Rothschild maintains that naturalists are born and not made. When she initiated wild flower and grass cultivation – which is increasingly fashionable – she did so primarily to encourage the conservation of the wonderful flora of the countryside. And she believes that the green of the foliage, the star-like flowers in the grass with their mingled scents in summer, bring to us peace of mind and a sense of the spiritual serenity which has rolled down the years from the time of the Garden of Eden.

WHEN HER FAMILY ask Princess Sturdza what she wants for her birthday, every year the reply is the same: cow-manure. Her garden at Vasterival, near Dieppe, is her life and her passion, a place where acres of precious and rare plants thrive. Many are sent to her from botanical gardens and by collectors around the world, thanks to the connections she has made with her impressive horticultural life. Vice President of the Royal Horticultural Society, President of the International Dendrology Society and one of the few non-English recipients of the prestigious Gold Veitch Memorial Medal for outstanding contributions to art, science and agriculture, Princess Sturdza has created one of the most extensively planted gardens anywhere. Didier Willery, who has spent nearly seven years photographing Vasterival every month, estimates that there are over eleven thousand different plant varieties flourishing in the garden. Botanists from all over the world visit, often bringing rare gifts, such as a six-metre-wide spreading prunus, a unique tree from Japan, breathtakingly beautiful when in flower. The garden also boasts six hundred and fifty different varieties of rhododendron and azalea.

The plants in her garden grow, mature, die and return to the earth as nourishment for the soil. Compost heaps of lawn clippings, twigs, pulverized bark and fallen leaves are conveniently positioned around the nine hectares of the garden. This natural food reserve – a wonderful mulch which lies several centimeters thick over the entire garden – is the secret of the plants' luxurious beauty. 'A shilling for the plant, ten shillings for the planting' is Greta Sturdza's motto. Once a tree or a shrub is in place, that is not the end of her job. A top blanket of mulch is spread as a protection from frost, from drying out, and as a deterrent for weeds. I think she was one of the first French gardeners even to use the word 'mulch'. She simply doesn't see any point in using chemicals in a well-planted, well-tended garden.

THE ORGANIC PIONEER

◆

VASTERIVAL
DIEPPE, FRANCE

PRINCESS STURDZA

This is what Princess Sturdza calls 'La chambre bleue', planted with her special selection of Vasterival hydrangeas of the most intense, electrifying blue. In the acid, heavily mulched soil, the mop-head flowers of exceptional size remain on the plant for a long period.

Opposite A typical summer scene in a bog-like valley, where a strong-growing variety of astilbe thrives. This is another special product of Vasterival's gardens, and is planted in bold clusters under the semi-shade of deciduous trees.

A background of *Erica arborea alpina*, a plant which can reach almost two metres in height, is a dramatic foil for the brilliant flowers of *Rhododendron* 'Elizabeth Jenny', a neat, compact, ground-hugging variety.

Planting is carried out on a four-layer basis: overhead, the trees; under the trees, the shrubs; beneath or around the shrubs, ground-cover plants; under the ground cover, bulbs. This scheme ensures a yearly cycle of growth and colour. The placing of the right plant in the right place is her prime concern, as the land is very varied. Whole areas have been devoted to special planting schemes, of which there is a bewildering variety, each one taking into consideration the special needs of the plants and allowing for seasonal colour. Plants are lifted and divided every two years to avoid overcrowding and to keep them disease-free. She pays special attention to the design of colour schemes and to the flowering height of the various plants. The Michaelmas daisy border, a riot of pinks and blues, can rival Gertrude Jekyll's border at Munstead.

Close by the house, a retaining dry-stone wall with grit as a planting medium is clothed in special alpine plants which need complete drainage and poor soil. This is the home of rare Asian orchids which don't normally flourish out of doors. Because this is a dry spot, many precious bulbs can be grown, along with a collection of primroses which have to be lifted and divided each year to prevent their degeneration. A fervent lover of magnolias, the Princess cultivates around eighty different varieties, including the impressive *Magnolia dawsoniana*, over fifteen metres tall, with flowers measuring thirty-five centimetres across. It took seventeen years to produce its first flower, just one on its topmost branch, but now it is a mass of bloom for several weeks at the end of March.

Special walks are plotted around the garden to show the various plantings at their best. There are two walks for each month of the year. For example, in February, when other gardens seem drab, Vasterival has a glorious show of rhododendrons. The *Rhododendron* 'Praecox', usually a small variety, here measures two metres high and four wide, its little mauve flowers covering the branches, which have already shed their leaves. The next to flower are *Rhododendron williamsianum*, their pink flowers paling as the weeks go by. The large red *Rhododendron* 'Cynthia' have been planted in such a way as to appear like a series of flowering cascades, the tallest being several metres high. The winter perfumed walk of *Viburnum farreri* and *Viburnum x bodnantense*, is captivating, with the shrubs' branches pinned down to ensure a graceful curve during the flowering months.

Bog plants and shade-loving plants are situated where they will grow best and not to suit the whims of the gardener. Nothing looks contrived or forced; rather, plants look comfortable in their surroundings. This effect is in part achieved by restricted planting, so that the plants do not suffer from overcrowding and can grow and spread freely. Since this is an ecological garden, great care is taken to avoid disease and contamination – all rose prunings and diseased cuttings are burned and a sickly-looking plant is placed in a nursery-bed to recuperate.

Many plants are propagated at Vasterival from cuttings or seeds. These are some of the Princess's special treasures: particularly the bluest of blue hydrangeas, 'Vasterival', which in years to come we will be able to grow in our own gardens. Hellebores are another species almost synonymous with Vasterival. The wonderful damp, acid soil of the surrounding woodland suits their needs. Special attention is paid to the hellebores, and their leaves are carefully removed when the flowers appear to ensure a more dramatic effect and healthier plants. From December onwards, whole borders of hellebores appear around the shrubs. Patches of the snow-white *Helleborus orientalis* variety surround clumps of blood-red

Helleborus orientalis and *Helleborus niger* are planted in well-spaced clusters in a heavy mulch that ensures a maximum flowering performance. The bright red stems of *Cornus alba* are cut right back each season, producing a fresh growth of branches over a metre tall.

stems of *Cornus alba* 'Westonbirt', kept spectacularly red by an annual pruning out of the mature stems.

Banks of heather, winding trails perfumed by a carpet of daphne, winter-flowering *Hamamelis mollis* 'Pallida' with the palest of yellow flowers, contrasting with *Hamamelis x intermedia* 'Diane', the reddest of all, are a joy to witness. In a low, narrow valley, a stream of *Iris kaempferi* (originating from Japan) does wonders in the damp, acid soil, where the flowers lift their flat colourful heads well above their leaves. Later on, drifts of astilbes from the palest of pinks to the brightest of reds edge the stream. Along the woodland paths, the bluest hydrangeas, the 'Vasterival' variety with their impressive flower-heads, smother the hillsides. The most spectacular is a dome-shaped plant of perfect proportions over three and a half metres wide, flowering over a low carpet of heather.

To enjoy the roses at Vasterival, you just have to lift up your head, as they grace the trees and range over shrubs; the variety *Rosa* 'Albertine', for example, scrambles up an apple tree. Another apple tree is host to the pink flowering *Rosa* 'Olivier Vibert', chummed up with a *Clematis* 'Perle d'Azur'. The rose 'New Dawn' and the pink *Clematis* 'Niobe' make another pretty picture. The rampant 'Kiftsgate' rose has already devastated a couple of pine trees and is now being closely watched and even pruned. A special area around the tennis court, where the Princess entertains her friends to tea, is mostly devoted to herbaceous planting and to many rose varieties. The plants are spectacular: the phlox are two metres tall; the alstroemaria more profuse than in other gardens; the towering blue aconitum more robust and taller than elsewhere. The secret is, of course, the mulch applied generously to every border in the autumn.

An island bed of colour for spring in which *Narcissus pseudonarcissus*, *Prunus mume* and heathers weave around a *Hydrangea* 'Vasterival' that retains its dry flower heads – which will only be removed in spring after the frosts are over.

Above Warm autumn tints are apparent in a woodland area of the garden planted with *Viburnum plicatum* 'Vasterival'. *Below* The flaky, papery bark of *Betula grossa* gives interest even when this deciduous tree is not in leaf. Clever pruning ensures the shape and the peeling of each branch.

The garden's trees are Greta's pride and joy, and many of them are not only beautiful, but they are also rare. Among the most spectacular is the *Cornus controversa* 'Variegata', whose branches grow out horizontally in flat waves of pale yellow and white leaves. Training her trees to produce interesting shapes is an art the Princess has cultivated over the years and which is remarkably well demonstrated by an *Exochorda korolkowii*, where the lower branches have been removed so that it is beautifully laden with flowers in the early spring. A number of the trees are planted for their lovely coloured barks. The shiny orange trunks of *Prunus maackii*, the *Prunus serrula* with ringed bark like polished mahogany and the silver trunk of birch (*Betula pendula*) show up against the winter-flowering, perfumed mahonia. This woodland scene is then studded with jewel-like *Cyclamen coum* and *Cyclamen neapolitanum*.

In spite of much tribulation and many setbacks, such as the storm in 1978 when a hundred and sixty trees were uprooted, then the winter of 1989 when the temperature went down to -21°C and forty-two superb cypress were blown down, and, to crown it all, twenty-seven invasions of wild boar, the garden survives. Greta Sturdza believes that she has achieved her goal of creating a four-seasons garden thanks to very strict rules: thorough preparation of the soil before planting; regular mulching of every plant; the pruning out of dead branches from trees and shrubs; and resisting the temptation to undertake new planting until the existing garden is properly tended.

The garden at Vasterival is of major importance as a harbinger of the ideas and techniques which will become fashionable and even essential in the twenty-first century. The quality and diversity of this truly organic, plantswoman's garden are indeed a model and an inspiration for future gardeners.

CHYVERTON IS A FIVE-HUNDRED-ACRE woodland estate in Cornwall. Although it was designed and planted in 1770 by the then owner, John Thomas, it is Chyverton's more recent plantings and gardening style, undertaken by its present owner, Nigel Holman, which earn it a place as an inspiration for gardeners of the twenty-first century.

Chyverton is situated on the windy Cornish peninsula. Mass planting of oak, acer, ash, beech, sycamore and flowering classes of rhododendrons – some now attaining the size of six by eight metre trees – mean that Chyverton is no longer an exposed, windswept plain, but a protected environment for some of the most difficult plants to establish. The estate's twenty acres of planted woodland are partitioned into twenty-nine recesses, which form windbreaks. In 1924, when Treve Holman, father of the present owner, acquired Chyverton, he set about planting twenty acres of rhododendrons, magnolias, acers, amongst which are many rare species which still flourish today. Nigel Holman doesn't worry much about hardiness, explaining his philosophy that if you plant well, the plants respond. The good-planting theory is proved by the sight of a thriving *Magnolia macrophylla dealbata* from Mexico, with its three-foot-long leaves, or of one of the finest specimens of *Styrax japonica*, smothered in clusters of dainty bell-flowers.

One rare treasure follows on from another, a *Lanaria ferruginea*, a *Drimys lanceolata*. All are situated in ankle-deep grass, with no defined paths and no laid-out borders. In Nigel's gardening life, weeding is a useless time consumer and a great disturbance to plant life. He just ignores chemicals and keeps things in shape with a lawnmower, in and out of the recesses, chopping off any unwelcome vegetation, with the result that the grass is just long

NATURE TAKES ITS COURSE

◆

CHYVERTON
CORNWALL,
ENGLAND

NIGEL HOLMAN

Among the grasses, dainty flowers of wild parsley invade the edge of the pond, which in turn reflects the overhanging, purple-leaf beech.

Previous pages There is a bridge, therefore a stream, albeit invisible, but the plants tell of its presence with clusters of *Primula japonica* and ferns backed by broad-leafed *Lysichiton camtschatcensis*, which will burst into white flowering swathes in early spring.

Over a hundred years old, this giant oak, vanquished by a storm, was allowed to lie in peace. Full of vitality, it burrowed into the earth, setting down new roots, and again is in full leaf.

enough to allow primroses, orchids and bluebells to carpet the land. Leaves are never swept up – God forbid – so the plants mulch themselves and each other. Weeds are not destroyed; even a crop of nettles is simply mown down and left to rot *in situ*. It is with such good husbandry that a very old garden is allowed to express itself and attain indefinite rejuvenation.

Trees put out lower branches which will tend to root as they touch the ground, a layering process usually hampered by the gardeners' weeding and hoeing. At Chyverton, plants are layering like mad: *Viburnum plicatum* 'Mariesii' shows off its numerous 'petticoats', each one taking root away from the parent plant to form a new young shrub. And if an old magnolia tree falls down, Nigel just looks at it, sympathises with its predicament, advises it to carry on and make a new start, and leaves it to root in peace.

At Chyverton, the will to live and to encroach upon the land is creating the most beautiful of natural scenes. Once, Nigel's mother planted a myrtle hedge to protect her much-loved herbaceous border. Today, the myrtles are over twenty feet tall and their cinnamon-coloured bark and evergreen foliage form a protective wall running down to the riverbank. Here, magnolias flower from season to season: in March, huge clusters of pink flowers on *Magnolia campbellii*; in April, pale pink goblets on *Magnolia x soulangeana*; and, finally, the early summer variety of *Magnolia hypoleuca* flowers in June with its heavily fragrant, butter-coloured flowers.

Chyverton boasts over two hundred different varieties of magnolia. It will soon be able to boast some of the rarest plants from China, where Nigel visited on a plant-hunting expedition to collect seed. He says it was his dream come true. The joy of receiving and

planting his own seedlings in a year or two – they are being propagated by specialist nurseries – will be an exciting achievement; even if some fail, the fittest will survive.

Plants at Chyverton are not fed, pruned or staked and many have attained exceptional stature: the *Styrax japonica* – known as the snowball tree – is one of the largest in Britain. The garden is a cultivated wilderness, where the rare and the not-so-rare form a harmonious picture. A rare Bhutan pine and the dainty-leafed, autumn-coloured *Acer palmatum* 'Atropurpureum', an exceptionally rare Huon pine (*Lagarostrobus franklinii*) from Tasmania and more viburnum, layer in total disregard of their neighbours. The *Rhododendron* 'Cornish Red' is a typical inhabitant of local gardens, only here we see one accomplishing an exceptional feat, the ardent red trusses clambering almost twenty metres up its host tree. Rhododendrons have always behaved in such a fashion – if one lets them – sprawling their russet branches around to root, and to ensure new life. Layering is the almost magical survival recipe. A great giant oak, probably three hundred years old and with a trunk measuring about ten metres in circumference, lies sprawled across a clearing. It is a great beauty as it takes root along its branches. I am sure Nigel has a word of gratitude each time he passes by – his plants are his friends, whose daily life he shares.

As in most Cornish gardens, a stream winds its way between banks of ferns and *Primula japonica*. Lush patches of lysichiton indicate the water's course, while orchids raise their heads between the grasses. A Monet-style bridge is quite a surprise, but as I put my hand on the wooden rail, I am surprised to find tufts of mosses invading the timber. It needs Nigel Holman's authority and vigilance to keep his plants in check and to encourage those that lag behind to ensure that Chyverton is a constantly developing garden.

Rain and humid air are the ideal conditions for rhododendrons to flourish, the proof given by this outstanding 'Cornish Red', of which Nigel is rightly proud.

CHAPTER TWO

INSPIRED BY SCIENCE

THIS CHAPTER CONCENTRATES on a single, remarkable garden, one which is uniquely concerned with the core issues of contemporary scientific inquiry. The story of the creation of the universe and our place within it is slowly being decoded by scientists, and this garden sets out to prove that man's role in interpreting his universe is more important than ever. The garden is not merely a scientific exposé, as its aim is to be as beautiful as it is instructive. As a result, many disciplines – including engineering, hydraulics, astronomy and botany – have played a part in its creation. It has become a place where art and wit, and science and technology, are inseparable.

Opposite A Chinese-style, red-painted wooden walkway snakes between two ornamental bridges in Charles Jencks' Scottish garden. Each bridge is equipped with a platform from which to view different aspects of the garden.

Below The 'Ambiguity' of this inscription is borne out by the fact that the word can be read from either direction, as becomes clear if you turn this book upside down.

A COSMOLOGICAL LANDSCAPE

◆

BORDERS, SCOTLAND

CHARLES JENCKS

The so-called 'Black Hole Platform' is designed as a terrace for *al fresco* meals. It represents the way in which a black hole warps time and space with the intense pull of its gravity. The feature is made out of a chequerboard of aluminium and Astroturf.

I HAD BEEN TOLD that if I was not familiar with cosmogenics, Asian culture and the science of complexity, I would not be equipped to appreciate Charles Jencks' and his late wife Maggie Keswick's garden. But as I stood in the Scottish hills, with a distant haze around me and a new gardening language unfolding in front of my eyes, I realized that the issue was not one of familiarity, but rather one of concentration and of a willingness to think and to understand. Charles Jencks and Maggie Keswick started work on these gardens in 1989. Sadly, in 1993 Maggie had a recurrence of cancer and died in 1995. She was largely responsible for the lakes, he for the mounds and twists, but they worked together on most things, sometimes, says Charles, 'with passionate disagreement, but always with great pleasure'. Charles is expanding their project alone as a tribute to his wife, in memory of their work together.

The same vocabulary cannot be used to describe Charles and Maggie's garden as would be used to describe others. Certainly, an extraordinary sense of calm and inevitability

A plan drawing of part of the garden shows the breaks in symmetry that are the secret of the story of the creation of the universe. It also shows the linked locations of the Black Hole Platform and the Symmetry Break Terrace.

prevails in this environment: it is impossible to define where landscape ends and the garden begins. The feeling here is of invigorating, surrealistic beauty, linked to an inescapable sense of logic. There is much interest today in cosmology and chaos theory and in others of the sciences which can be characterized as 'non-linear dynamics', so named because, taken as a whole, they challenge the previous world view, the mechanistic interpretation of nature. This is a garden which represents nothing less than the story of the universe, not from the point of view of the planting, nor from a religious or historical angle, nor a Darwinian perspective, but by translating into a visual formula these new scientific preoccupations. The challenge Jencks undertakes is to represent this dynamic scientific process in a valid, static horticultural vision.

The 'Symmetry Break Terrace' is a visual metaphor for the four 'jumps' over 15 billion years that resulted in the creation and life of the universe.

Viewed from the Snail Mound, the grassland twists away in similar mound shapes that in turn form the edges of the paisley-shaped water features.

The Soliton Wave Gate is one of several such gates that represent energy, trapped in the twists.

Feeling that traditional landscape design was over exploited, its formulae too familiar, Charles and Maggie turned to new sources of inspiration. Maggie's in-depth knowledge of Chinese geomancy revealed a very apt metaphor for interpreting the local Scottish landscape of deep, smooth valleys, low hills and long curving mounds. Chinese landscape painters, following the teachings of Taoist monks and philosophers, saw hills and mountains as the 'bones of the earth' energized with the 'vital breath' of subterranean dragons. Similar ideas were employed here for a set of five different gardens. The individual gardens are themselves linked by large, linear forms representing those found in nature, such as worms, snakes and snails, or by abstract twisting lines. The whole vision is based on the assumption that nature's basic forms are continuously changing and that they are curved.

A mixture of practicality and aesthetic preconception is evident in these large swathes of landscape. A grassed spiral mound about fifty feet high and a series of mounds four hundred feet long and twisting like a snake are reflected in paisley-shaped 'mirrors', the ponds. The snake mounds first twist towards the main pond, then continue in the opposite direction through a series of terraces, towards another garden and a quite different vista. There is a vital energy and movement in these contours and in the paisley shapes of the ponds which reflect them.

The snail mound emerges from two separate spirals, one forming the head and the other the tail. Because the two spirals are at an oblique angle to the ground, they create the paradoxical aspect of both rising and falling in ascent: in order to walk up this horticultural sculpture, you have to go down; and when you walk down, you have to go up. This phenomenon is designed as a sort of aerial labyrinth and is meant to be frustrating, enough so to make you think about the difficulty of moving towards a goal.

A more formal 'Physics Garden', with models of an atom, of Gaia, of the universe and of several other cosmogenic elements, is under construction. A model of the DNA double helix, built in different materials – from aluminium to wood to grass – is at the centre of an area of planting devised to represent a cell. Such features of the garden were designed following advice from scientists, metalworkers and other experts and, says Jencks, 'they interpret the truths of the universe through displaced and combinatorial models. They are not illustrations of contemporary science but re-imaginations of what this public discourse tells us. It is important to stress the difference.'

A colour plan of the Physics Garden, a kitchen garden designed to represent the six senses: the usual five, complemented by a sixth – anticipation.

An overview of the Physics Garden is dominated by a sculpture of the DNA double helix. There is, nevertheless, culinary as well as metaphorical meaning here, evidenced by the neat arrangements of salad plants.

The significant, sculpted inscription 'Synthesis' can also be read from both directions.

As new garden design theories emerge, it is difficult to predict whether or not this dynamic scientific conception will become dated, or even obsolete, or whether it will just take its place as one amongst the famous gardens around the world. Jencks concludes that 'science is irreversible, cumulative and progressive and man's role in interpreting the universe is a worthwhile aim for designers of all disciplines'. He believes that garden design, like architecture, must reflect new sciences because they are set to reveal the deeper, formative principles of nature. Certain other contemporary designers also feel the need for an entirely new approach to garden design, but have taken the easy way out; they have simply reduced the landscape to a blank canvas of what might already be there. So far, scientific approaches to garden creation have been shy and sporadic, as if no one has dared or bothered to formulate new ideas, let alone to theorize. Charles Jencks delves deeper. He studies nature's basic forms and unites the wider language of the universe with the inner language of art, thus developing the range of the aesthetic. 'In all of this work,' says Jencks, 'I am convinced it is as much the inspiration of recent science and its various new languages as it is we who are designing. It is an approach which makes the development of a new grammar of architecture and landscape as much a discovery as an invention.'

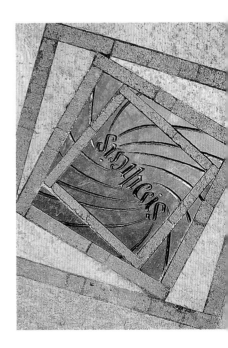

CHAPTER THREE

THE PLANT LOVERS

A NEW SOCIAL PHENOMENON has emerged in the gardening world – that of specialist plant shows, not only in England, but also on the Continent. There is hardly a locality which doesn't have a garden club or association, or organize a plant fair or sale. They have become social events to which more and more people flock in search of something special, something which they hope that their neighbour doesn't have. In the forefront at these events are talented professional gardeners promoting rare plants and colour themes for garden design.

Plants from far-off lands – China, Mexico, South Africa, India and many other countries – are pouring into European gardens via small specialized nurseries and well-equipped garden centres. As a result of these outlets, we will see an increasing number of plantsman's gardens, not only those created by professional designers, but also those made by dedicated garden lovers whose hobby is visiting gardens, perusing gardening books, propagating their own treasures and acquiring and nurturing new plants.

Opposite Flourishing *Alchemilla mollis* edges the long vista of the gravel path at Sticky Wicket garden in Dorset. The absinthe-coloured flowers will last all through the summer.

Right Originally from Tibet, the puffy flowers on graceful wands of *Thalictrum delavayi* are mixed in with a denser planting of *Catananche caerulea*.

A HOME FOR WILDLIFE

◆

STICKY WICKET
DORSET, ENGLAND

PETER & PAM LEWIS

STICKY WICKET LIES DEEP in the beautiful Dorset countryside at Blackmore Vale. The garden was so named because of the previous owners' association with the local cricket team, although Peter and Pam Lewis, the present owners, suspect the name might have been chosen on account of the garden's sticky clay soil, four acres of rough pasture surrounding the house. The Lewises' aim was to create a garden that would be as inspiring aesthetically as it would be attractive to the wildlife they wanted to support. Their plants are carefully selected with these aims in mind and many are cottage garden favourites – often those with herbal virtues or with romantic or symbolic associations. The garden is managed on organic principles and no harmful chemicals are used.

Peter and Pamela Lewis see an urgent need to conserve our British native plants and habitats. It is known that among the remaining three per cent of natural habitat meadows in the country, very few are clay meadows, which are more difficult to establish because of the extreme fertility of the soil. The Lewises have created tiny 'sample meadows' in their garden to test seed response in such clay conditions.

Flowering in late summer and autumn, *Eryngium planum*, with its wine-red heads, mingles with the bulbs of *Allium sphaerocephalon*. Both can be dried and are therefore very popular with flower arrangers.

This is an unusual, fibrated variety of *Papaver somniferum*.

Opposite Always a good background plant, the silver-leafed, perfumed artemisia is teamed with diascia, an almost ever-flowering perennial that often retains colour right into the winter, spreading rapidly. Island beds are set out here amongst the weaving gravel paths.

Grasses mingle effectively with herbaceous plants in a border or make a show on their own. Here *Hordeum jubatum* and *Lagurus ovatus* are magical in the setting sun.

The garden is designed in such a way that the planting of each area focuses on a specific wildlife theme. The Frog Garden, in shades of blue and yellow, has a pond as the main feature and is to be further enlarged and developed in response to the enthusiastic approval of the frogs. The Bird Garden is designed in a way that allows ample opportunity to marvel at the increasing number of species that visit the garden. Colours from pastel pinks and lavender blues through to crimson and violet spin together in the Round Garden. Colour is used as a tool to create an illusion of perspective and the colours are orchestrated to ebb and flow in intensity, rather than to create any strong contrasts. The large, open, sunny site makes it particularly attractive to butterflies and bees and other beneficial insects. The White Garden, or 'white wilderness', encompasses all aspects of wildlife gardening and especially reflects the couple's passion for wild flowers.

A large proportion of the planting throughout the garden is gravel based; as self-seeding is encouraged, the plants then have good protection from waterlogging. Willow plays an important role, whether as a foil for the flowers, for making fences, as a protective hut for ducks and poultry, or to create the magical sculptural appearance of a dear old lady leaning on her stick. I asked Pamela to what ripe old age the lady could aspire? It appears that to keep up appearances, like other ladies, she has a 'lift' and fresh make-up every year or so.

Clad in willows and grasses, a white witch with long flaxen hair makes her way through a secluded wood.

Opposite The dark wine-coloured *Antirrhinum barrellieri* 'Black Prince' and *Diascia rigescens* are an interesting combination. The diascia will make a good show for almost six months and will often keep its leaves in winter.

S ANDRA AND NORI POPE had already created a number of fine gardens from their home base on Vancouver Island, off the west coast of Canada, when they were tempted to travel halfway across the globe to create a garden for themselves in the sleepy Somerset countryside. They were attracted by the challenge posed by a neglected site of unfriendly, alkaline clay back in 1986. The result of their considerable labours, at the turn of the centuries, is one of the most famous gardens in Western Europe, based on a pure vision of colour in the ideal garden.

Nori Pope inveighs with feeling against what he calls 'colour noise' – a horticultural attack on the eye by a mindless mix of contrasting, and often mutually destructive, battles for attention between plants in the average border. A passion for colour at its finest has become the basis of the couple's design at Hadspen.

They feel strongly that there has never been a better time to garden, because of the availability of an enormous number of plants, those which are now being fed into the gardening world by botanists, plant hunters and breeders. For gardeners, this unprecedented range of species is one of the most significant developments of the last decades of the twentieth century, opening up new aesthetic possibilities for the creation of unusual and subtle colour effects.

The garden at Hadspen House consists of two hectares set against a magnificent background of mature trees that rise on a hill above the former kitchen garden. It is here, against a long, curved wall, that the Popes have brought their vision to life with a planting which runs from the hottest colours in the spectrum to the coolest along the entire hundred-metre length of the wall. The individual flowers which make up their painter's palette have been selected with the greatest care for their precise colours, and some of them have even been specially hybridized by Nori Pope. The overall effect, changing with the seasons, is magical. Dominant colours are carefully punctuated with plants of contrasting colour. A yellow bank of rudbekia, evening primrose (*oenothera*) and potentilla will have as its counterpoint the blue of a solitary lupin, a scabious or a patch of cat-mint.

PAINTING
WITH FLOWERS

◆

HADSPEN HOUSE
SOMERSET, ENGLAND

SANDRA & NORI POPE

Opposite Tulipa bifloriformis 'Black Parrot' grows at the edge of a group of *Cynara cardunculus*, providing a wonderful contrast of colours.

Below The double yellow borders in the walled garden, planted with numerous species, including grasses, verbascum, lupin, fennel and potentilla.

Above, from left to right
Individual species at Hadspen
House: *Alcea rugosa*;
Oenothera biennis; *Dahlia*
'David Howard'; *Kniphofia*
triangularis; *Dahlia* 'Bishop of
Llandaff'; *Potentilla* 'Gibson's
Scarlet'; *Scabiosa* 'Ace of
Spades'; and *Angelica*
atropurpurea.

In this view of the curved borders, the strong reds, oranges and
purples of the planting schemes are evident. Part of the colourful
vegetable garden is seen in the foreground.

Both the Popes have had a fine art training, but it is Sandra who has the expert colourist's eye: she knows exactly what she needs to complement a grouping of flowers. She will examine a colour effect in the border and see it needs an extra note to enhance the overall result. She will then ask Nori to make, for example, a hollyhock exhibiting a deeper apricot shade than usual. He will set to work to produce what has turned out to be, in this case, *Alcea rosea* 'Peach', one of his hybridizing successes, now available in garden centres. He has also produced the lovely dark *Astrantia*, 'Hadspen Blood', the really golden *Dicentra* 'Gold Heart', and the *Dahlia merckii alba*.

Sandra has now requested that her husband make a deep red-maroon flowering fennel. Not every wife can order presents with such precision . . . and get them. She explains her reasons for being demanding: 'An important aspect of any planting at Hadspen is that it must perform for at least seven months of the year, maintaining not just the colour of the area but also the general ambience, the rhythm and the mood to create a picture that may change in form from season to season, but not in content. The tulip 'Red Shine' is replaced by *Papaver orientale* 'Beauty of Livermere', which is followed by the dahlia 'Bishop of Llandaff'. Once the poppies are finished, they are cut to the ground, annuals or half-hardy perennials are planted close in, and the poppy foliage sprouts up again around them. Phlox, soapwort and lychnis are pinched out by a third in April to stagger their flowering and encourage them to continue over months, instead of weeks. Every visible sliver of earth is planted with bulbs, perennials, annuals, shrubs and climbers.'

This wonderfully attractive couple have added something new to the art of gardening at Hadspen with their imaginative use of every growing thing that comes to hand – herbaceous plants, roses, shrubs and even fruit and vegetables. It is the triumph of the educated eye.

Below, from left to right
Further individual species include *Alcea rosea* 'Nigra'; *Allium sphaerocephalon*; *Geranium psilostemon*; *Cosmos bipinnatus* 'Pink'; *Lavatera trimestris* 'Silver Cup'; *Potentilla x hopwoodiana*; *Alcea* 'Chater's Double Apricot'; and *Rosa* 'Sally Holmes'.

NEW AND LAVISH GARDENS are now being created in parts of the world where planting gardens is a virtually unknown art. Better communications, economic expansion, accumulation of fame, wealth and ambition have led some people to seek virgin retreats further afield than ever before. Fleeing established civilization to recreate an even more highly civilized way of life has enabled a happy, growing minority to plant some of the most lavishly mature gardens, many of which will live well into the twenty-first century. The owners' quest is for privacy and beauty and it is doubtful whether they even know that these gardens contain some of the most sought-after, and some of the rarest, plants in the world.

One of these secluded retreats, on a Caribbean island, posed considerable problems to the creation of an exotic garden. Heavy, mechanized equipment was not available on the island where the garden was to be designed, and the techniques resorted to were similar to those used by the Ancient Egyptians, or even by the makers of Stonehenge. Dynamite was used during the construction of the swimming pool to break boulders set in the ground, but because of the lack of expertise in its use, it was not employed elsewhere in the garden. Instead, the age-old practice of burning fires to heat the boulders and then throwing water on them to break them was revived. This worked quite well, but had to be done over and over again, as the boulders broke off in layers, much like the peel and pith of an orange.

TROPICAL EXOTICA
◆
THE CARIBBEAN

Opposite This spectacular swimming pool goes one better than Hollywood. *Below* Frangipani, a slender tree native of the West Indies, has fragrant, long-lasting flowers.

Left The banyan tree – a native of India – is the same species as the *Ficus elastica*, or rubber, we use as a house plant. In the tropics, a single tree can cover large areas by sending down branches which root, producing large trunks that in turn also root.

Above A grove of stately royal palms. In more temperate climes, we use smaller specimens as indoor container plants.

Right Bougainvillea, a spiny, vigorous vine native to Brazil, has inconspicuous summer flowers surrounded by brilliantly coloured bracts about an inch long. Bougainvillea can also be grown in milder climates, where it is useful as an evergreen to cover walls and trellises.

Above Dracaena, whose silhouette has given it the common name 'Crown of Thorns'. Many varieties of dracaena are used as pot plants in colder climates, but do not then reach tree form.

One of the most persistent problems of the site was the lack of open land, free of stone, in which to plant. The most sensible plan of action here eventually seemed to be to bury the stone boulders deep enough to be able to plant over the top, rather than use these primitive methods to try to remove them. A back-hoe was used to dig a hole as deep as possible, about fifteen feet, beside a boulder. Then the boulder was pushed into the hole and covered over with the earth which had been removed. The ground was levelled or terraced as required, and then digging could start in another area of the garden. Later, topsoil was brought in and the planting started. This system proved very successful in creating walkways in grass from the houses at the top of the garden, reaching down to the beach. The grassed areas were designed to radiate outwards from the houses like the fingers of a hand, giving an expansive feel and lovely views to the sea.

The extreme heat and dryness of the island's climate meant that fresh water was scarce. The answer to this problem was the desalination of the sea, but this was a complicated technical feat, since the salt water had to be piped up to the property to a filtering system. Judging by the lush beauty of the plants and greenness of the lawn now, the system works. With adequate watering and plenty of sun, the plants perform dramatically, enabling a mature-looking garden to blossom in almost the first year of its planting.

The paths were laid with natural stone, mined and cut on the island, designed so that none should be straight for more than a few metres, but that all should be slightly curved, to add interest. The beauty of a plant is much more apparent on a curved area, where it will stand out from its neighbours, than it is on a straight path, where the eye will automatically go for the vista instead. Curved paths also allow an element of surprise and make a garden appear denser and bigger. It is nice to come across something you didn't expect: a gazebo, a swimming pool, a friendly seat, as you wind your way around a garden.

Codiaeum are variegated shrubs, or 'crotons', popular as conservatory or house plants in colder climates.

A dense, rampant ground-cover plant – locally called 'ground orchid' because of its long narrow leaves and flower emerging at basal height – is planted in a circular bed amongst the rocks.

THE PLANT HUNTERS

◆

COTHAY MANOR
SOMERSET,
ENGLAND

MARY-ANNE &
ALISTAIR ROBB

WHEN MARY-ANNE AND ALISTAIR ROBB acquired their Somerset home, the garden was just a series of empty, albeit mature, hedged rooms. But what could be more practical and attractive to dedicated plant lover Mary-Anne than these protected areas in which to grow rare and lovely plants? For several years, she had been passionately plant hunting in South Africa, Spain, Turkey and on the border of Russia and Persia. She has introduced many new species from her expeditions into the six separate enclosures of Cothay's garden and she is now actively creating more planting space. A bog garden, a cottage garden, a terrace and courtyard area have been added and now include many of the new treasures.

The collecting is a true labour of love. 'There is nothing,' says Mary-Anne, 'that brings back the ecstatic emotion of being in love like the glow that pervades the collector on acquiring a new treasure – a new plant.' Spending time with people who have a like-minded obsession, knowing that at the beginning of an expedition days stretch ahead in which you can endlessly discuss your latest botanical find, your passion for plants, is an enormous pleasure.

From the seventeenth century onwards, plant hunting has been gaining momentum. There are still thousands of plants out there, in Western Australia, the Himalayas and in China, which botanists are anxious to acquire. Intrepid, adventurous and dedicated, they have all left their mark on our landscapes and continue to do so. It was William Lobb who discovered the first Chilean monkey-puzzle tree (*Araucaria araucana*) and George Forest who brought back the bluest of blues, the flowering *Gentiana sino-ornata,* from the border of Tibet. The lovely golden May lily (*Maianthenum bifolium*) was found in Japan by John Veitch.

A young apprentice gardener from Scone Palace, David Douglas, set off to North America as a collector for the Horticultural Society of London, and among the thousands of treasures he collected were the cones of the Douglas fir tree, a conifer which now inhabits many of our forests. Sadly, Douglas's canoe was smashed to pieces in the Fraser River in Canada and he lost years of field notes. Eventually, he met a dramatic end, gored to death by a bull. Another great plant hunter, Sir Joseph Hooker, sent home eighty mule loads of plants and it is him we have to thank for the *Rhododendron dalhousiae*.

Opposite Onopordum acanthium is grown with *Campanula latiloba* in the centre foreground and *Nepeta faassenii* and *Anthemis punctata cupaniana* spill into the gravel. Wisteria grows up to the right of the gable, under planted with alstroemeria. *Below* A yew hedge runs along the herbaceous border, dominated by a white planting scheme.

This herbaceous border is dominated by *Echinacea pallida*. Mary-Anne Robb likes to concentrate her planting in sweeps of one colour broken up by white interplanting.

On one of her expeditions to South Africa, led by Martin Rix, Mary-Anne collected seeds of *Kniphofia northiae*, *Leonotis leonurus*, various dierama, *Felicia amelioides* and *Sutherlandia montana*. All these plants are quite familiar and established in the West, but it is still important to bring back new, indigenous seeds, as amongst them there could possibly be an unusual colour or a new form of the named variety. This is a little like looking for a needle in a haystack, but extremely rewarding when you come upon such a treasure. The seeds are sown back home, transplanted, and their flowering two or three years later awaited with much curiosity and anticipation.

Plant hunting has to be well timed, and Mary-Anne recalls the excitement of an expedition organized to see some spectacular desert bulbs which flower for barely two weeks of the year in Africa. There you might also spot a new form or an unusual colour. Brought back home by dedicated plant hunters, these newcomers won't all find their way into garden centres, but many of them will be picked up by small specialist nurseries, of which there are more and more around the country, catering for the private gardens of true plant lovers.

A quiet corner in the cherry garden shows the dominant colours blue and pink. This garden room, like others with different colour themes, is enclosed by a yew hedge. Although the general layout may appear classic, the planting is modern in its use of contrasting colours.

Below Rarely seen except in Mediterranean gardens, a group of *Michauxia tchihatchewii* is accompanied by sprays of verbena.

59

CHAPTER FOUR

ARTISTS IN THEIR GARDENS

FOR THE ARTIST – PAINTER, SCULPTOR OR CRAFTSMAN – creating a garden can be another way of interpreting creativity. Although many artists might deny their professional skills as garden designers, they often do possess the instinctive qualifications needed to create a garden – an eye for colour and form and a love of the natural world.

Many gardens designed at the turn of the century are more than simply decorative; rather, they are intended to be full of meaning and, in somewhat narcissistic times, that meaning is often about the self. The garden becomes an extension of self, and for the artist therefore also an extension of art, an important new area of a very private world. One artist turned gardener described the process thus: 'I like to be surrounded by my day-to-day paraphernalia, even in the garden. It's part of me, it's reassuring.'

Opposite At Little Sparta in Scotland, brightly coloured nymphs prance through the undergrowth. The artefacts in the garden contrast cleverly with the largely untamed scenery in which they are set.

Below At the LongHouse Foundation in the USA, Grace Knowlton's massive white masonry balls on the lawn show up dramatically against their green background.

61

BEAUTY, CONSERVATION, EDUCATION

◆

LONGHOUSE FOUNDATION NEW YORK STATE, USA

JACK LARSEN

In a spacious grass clearing, sculpture is positioned apparently at random, and is boldly dramatic in its simplicity. These bronze and masonry spheres created by Grace Knowlton may have a philosophical, as well as an aesthetic, significance for the artist.

JACK LENOR LARSEN IS AN ARTIST who closely observes ideas, colours and compositions during his constant travels abroad, and who later uses his impressions in the development of his garden at LongHouse. Larsen summarizes the intentions of his garden venture in three words: beauty, conservation and education.

An internationally renowned textile designer and one of the world's foremost authorities on traditional and contemporary crafts, Larsen created the LongHouse Foundation in 1992. The natural landscape was relatively flat before he took it in hand, using truckloads of sand excavated from the basement of the house to create dunes. He then covered the dunes with grasses to simulate real dunes on a beach. A pond was dug out and the earth piled behind the house to create a protective hill. He created changes in ground levels and pathways in what became a garden of exciting designs and innovative planting displays.

Flat slabs of stone salvaged from the river lead the way across the dunes, where planting has deliberately been kept sparse, in control, to make you feel as though you are walking along a river bed. In front of the house rises a stoney bank, where again the planting is in

Below Larsen is a collector of unusual artefacts, as long as they are made of noble materials. This massive wooden frame supporting a tall bell makes a fitting rustic object on the low, sandy gravel dunes.

Part of the arboretum that is Larsen's pride is planted with hundreds of rare cultivars, among clumps of daffodils, all in a mulch of bark. They help to create a woodland scene that is dotted with rocks, sculptures and indigenous shrubs.

A wide gravel area beside the house is the backdrop for an arrangement of flat stones and sculpted ceramic plaques decorated with strong abstract patterns.

perfect keeping with the landscape, with grasses and indigenous shrubs happy in poor, rough soil. There are also more sophisticated areas of the garden, where the dominant theme is monochrome planting: a white garden; a rose garden; an arboretum of several hundred rare trees, which is Larsen's pride.

One of his main preoccupations is to display species and cultivars which are compatible with the soil and weather conditions of the region. The show starts in spring with 220 cultivars of daffodils (underplanted with the blue *Vinca minor*), to which he adds 15,000 bulbs each year, imported from Holland and planted in great swathes along woodland walks, sometimes amongst massive natural boulders. Vistas are planned to be seen from the glass walls inserted between the piers of masonry around the house. A Japanese-style moon-viewing bridge links the house to the garden and overlooks a more formal, perennial border confined by granite-edged beds.

In his continuing search for unusual colours and plantings reminiscent of weaving techniques, Larsen finds much inspiration in nature. A field of golden day lilies or a carpet of all-season heather stimulates his creative appetite. His talents are many and his quest unending: he is a great traveller, a writer (he has eight books on textiles to his credit), he has revolutionized the textile industry by being the first to print on modern velvet, and he reigns over Larsen companies and showrooms in thirty different countries.

Jack Larsen is also an avid collector, fascinated by archaeology and by all handmade artefacts. Fate must have played a part when he built his house on piers, giving him an opportunity to display a collection of English staddle-stones. These interesting stone objects, wrongly considered eighteenth-century garden stools, were in fact extensively used in the fifteenth and sixteenth centuries as piers on which houses were built to keep out rodents. Today, the staddle-stones are grouped with some of sculptor Grace Knowlton's massive bronze and masonry spheres. It is wonderful to see sixteenth-century

An informal pebble patio area
is furnished with shrubs,
sculptures and other artefacts,
carefully positioned amongst
subtly coloured flower beds.

An avenue of red-painted, salvaged cedar wood posts is reminiscent of Japanese Shinto ceremonial gates.

and twentieth-century objects in perfect harmony. The sculpture already in the gardens is part of a growing programme; currently, permanent and long-term installations include, among others, works by Alfonso Ossorio, Claus Bury, Pavel Opecensky and St Gaudens. Larsen is striving, he says, to create a retreat of peace and beauty for future generations.

The house and the garden are developing into Larsen's own personal museum, where he can indulge in what has now become a mission. The objectives of the LongHouse Foundation reflect his professional interests and his desire to encourage creativity in gardening and in collecting and living with art. For him, every object has artistic potential. For example, a stack of rough cedar trunks salvaged from land clearance are planted as a parallel vista of posts leading to the woods. Then, to achieve a more dramatic impact, the posts are painted in the same blazing red-orange as the ceremonial Japanese Shinto gates, called *torii*. The surrounding planting is then planned to emphasize the brazen avenue, with its spring shrubbery of scarlet azaleas, red-leafed maples and purple prunus. The plants make a fiery impact, characteristic of Larsen's own temperament and his gift for colour and for transforming the everyday into art. A garden very often reflects the owner's personality and Jack Lenor Larsen's is no exception.

THE MAJORELLE GARDEN IS NOW Yves St Laurent's and Pierre Berger's Moroccan retreat. I met its creator, the artist Majorelle, in Morocco many years ago; he was sitting in his stall, bedecked with carpets, on the outskirts of an Arab souk, surrounded by his paintings – portraits of old Arab men, scenes from the souk, veiled fatmas, little Arab girls playing in the alleyways. I bought a picture from him of a whitewashed house with brilliant flowers in a pot on the doorstep. Sadly, I gave it away.

I remember Majorelle told me about his garden in Marrakesh where he would finally retire just 'to paint, to paint, to paint'. He died in 1962. Yves St Laurent and Pierre Berger discovered Majorelle's retreat at the end of a stoney dirt track leading from the market place in Marrakesh many years later. A wooden door in the fence opened into a wilderness of entangled, overgrown trees and a narrow path wound its way through the undergrowth. Suddenly, around a bend, appeared Majorelle's house and it was immediately apparent that this was the home of a painter. A burst of vivid blue walls with yellow windows and iron bars reflected the sunlight, a turquoise-painted pergola wrapped itself around the façade, adding to the exciting splash of colour. The balustrades were brushed green, the cement-laid paths became red, pink or blue, depending on the planting in the borders. Gates, windows and ironwork were clothed in bright yellow.

A fountain trickled into a blue pond in front of a kiosk protected by iron window casements. Such kiosks are called *moucharabia*, used by the women of the house to sit and see out without themselves being seen by passers-by. The feeling created is of being

A PAINTED
GARDEN

◆

MAJORELLE
MARRAKESH,
MOROCCO

YVES ST LAURENT

Walls, doorways and woodwork are painted in the vivid Majorelle blue found in many of the artist's paintings.

Left An exotic woodland setting planted with cacti and yucca surrounds a pond with a raised blue fountain.

Below Thanks to clever pruning, light penetrates this palm-tree forest, which still provides protection from the scorching Moroccan sun.

A patio-pergola runs the length of the house, where doors and windows boast the Majorelle blue. A painted, *trompe-l'oeil* effect has been created around the inset grille-windows.

'within' the picture of a painted garden. The house and garden, in the most avant-garde way, became an environmental canvas. Majorelle was the first painter to transform scenery into a living work of art, enabling him to live in his picture and not in front of it, totally surrounding himself with his decor.

Fervent gardeners both, Yves St Laurent and Pierre Berger decided to restore and bring to life Majorelle's home. In 1981, after years of neglect, the work began in a most organized way. Documents relating to the garden, such as photographs taken by friends and postcards made by a local photographer, were discovered. The original gardeners were tracked down, and they were able to provide an exact and detailed picture of the garden as it once was.

The vegetation was lush and overgrown. Bamboos, some from Malaysia, with green and white striped leaves, formed a rampart against the outside world, and the sound of water in the garden was a surprise under the African sun. The narrow paths were in red-painted cement, and heavenly perfumed pink and white datura hung their graceful blooms, stately glaucous yucca emerged among the sword leaves of *Chamaerops*, brilliant dracaena bunched together formed compact groups of striped leaves. The local rampant climber, bougainvillea, with its strident scarlet bracts, asserted itself wherever it could. Under the cover of a tall Egyptian papyrus, frogs and terrapins inhabited the ponds, swimming amongst the water lilies.

Now the garden is restored and much enhanced. A table is set for dinner in a marble courtyard surrounded by flowering laurels. In the distance, you can see the snow-clad Atlas mountains. It is in this setting that Yves St Laurent has designed some of his most beautiful clothes. Yves St Laurent and Pierre Berger have also created a museum of Moroccan art to ensure a link between Majorelle's work and that of other Moroccan artists. In the garden, the fountain plays sweetly and the muezzin calls to prayer, as he will for the next millennium.

Opposite Along this painted, covered walkway, a dramatic colour scheme is created by red cross bars resting on blue columns that retain shade from the overhanging trees.

A WALK THROUGH THE LASKETT is more than simply a stroll through a garden: it is a promenade through the memories of Sir Roy Strong and his wife Dr Julia Trevelyan Oman. At the outset, the garden was no more than a three-and-a-half-acre, triangular-shaped field in the Herefordshire countryside. The first impression of the garden now is of an overwhelming greenness in the innumerable hedges – consisting of beech, yew, Leyland cypress, box and prunus – which create long vistas and form intimate enclosures. They ensure that the garden retains shape and interest even in winter, and nearly all the enclosures are ornamentally paved with designs by Julia. She has created a kind of imaginative 'carpeting', formed from variously coloured, mosaiced stones. These floors visually link the enclosures and in spring are studded with bulbs that spell out the garden's colour themes. Julia is well equipped as the designer of these outdoor carpets: she studied at the Royal College of Art in London, and is a renowned set and costume designer, working with such prestigious clients as Covent Garden.

The house at The Laskett is painted bright yellow and blue, making it an important feature of the garden, with the yellow and blue theme reverberating out from the house in the choice of chairs, benches and decorative pyramids. Planting themes fan out from the house to the wider end of the triangular plot and appear to reach a crescendo in vistas that give onto colourful and intimate planted corners. Elsewhere, the formal layout is interrupted by vegetable and fruit plantings, as this is also the garden of gourmets. It is a haven for the vegetarian cook, with asparagus, carrots, leeks, Jerusalem artichokes and a variety of salad plants. A number of trees and bushes provide fruit for compotes, preserves and juices.

The garden tells the story of a marriage, of love and complicity, in a series of stage sets, many portraying Sir Roy's life and career as Director of the National Portrait Gallery and subsequently of the Victoria and Albert Museum in London, and as a broadcaster, writer

A GARDEN
AUTOBIOGRAPHY

◆

THE LASKETT
HEREFORDSHIRE,
ENGLAND

SIR ROY STRONG &
DR JULIA
TREVELYAN OMAN

Opposite In the Queen's Jubilee Garden, roses surround the sundial, a present from Sir Cecil Beaton. It is set in front of the Happiness Arch, inscribed 'He who plants a garden plants happiness'.

In the pavilion, a plaque designed by Simon Verity portraying Sir Roy between Queen Victoria and Prince Albert commemorates his resignation from the Victoria and Albert Museum.

Below In the natural grass meadow, backed by a yew hedge, is a recumbent stag with golden antlers.

With their entwined initials J and R, the simple box broderie set in gravel and flanked by stone urns is an apt symbol of the meaning of this garden. The lion statue (*left*) with its crown and shield stands in a planting of berberis.

Here is the plan of their story – The Laskett – laid out with vistas and beds, walks and rooms, hedges and shrubberies, terraces and fountains, orchards and topiary, temples and cats.
(Painting by Jonathan Myles-Lea)

and historian. In his published diaries, which cover the twenty years from 1967 to 1987, Sir Roy portrays himself as an eccentric, an aesthete, a gourmet of life, an inventive administrator fascinated by a society world which he was not born into, but to which he took like a duck to water once the opportunity was presented to him. Many of the major events of his working and social life have found expression in the garden at The Laskett.

Sir Roy laments the lack of historical records for the creation of some of the world's most interesting gardens, and has made sure that from the moment of its inception, the story of the making of The Laskett has been recorded in thorough archives, characteristic of this true historian. Every receipt has been kept, every design, thousands of photographs and, in recent years, the couple's gardening diaries and over ninety volumes of scrapbooks. Sir Roy does not claim to be a garden designer as such, but his several garden books have sold half a million copies worldwide and are certainly a source of ideas and inspiration for other gardeners.

The Laskett is sophisticated, exhibiting a firm touch of the baroque and the fine and precise tastes and talents of its owners. Classical themes are correct and respected but are presented with a quirk, a sense of humour, such as the coloured glass marbles threaded in between the knots of a formal knot garden. Sir Roy says that he and Julia 'didn't set out to make a grand garden, not even a big garden – but it seems to grow in spite of our commitment. If you asked what The Laskett garden was about, I might reply that it is the portrait of a marriage, the family we never had or wanted, a unique mnemonic landscape peopled with the ghosts of nearly everyone we have loved, both living and dead. It has always been conceived as an enclosed, private world, and that indeed is the key. There is no borrowed landscape. It deliberately shuts out the glory of the rolling hills of Herefordshire and remains a sealed, hermetic, magical domain of its own.'

I N BRAZIL, EVERYONE – not only high-profile citizens, but also taxi drivers, shopkeepers, waiters and civil servants – has heard of Roberto Burle Marx. They all seem proud of an artist whom they regard as a national icon. Burle Marx has probably made the largest and most varied contribution ever to his country's artistic life. His paintings hang in the National Museum of Fine Arts and he designed fabulous stage sets for the ballet and for carnival balls. His three-kilometre-long, swirling walkway of black, red and white stones and groups of trees constitutes one of the world's greatest promenades, the Copa Cabana beach walk, and he made important contributions as a landscape architect.

Burle Marx was born in Sao Paulo. His love of gardening and plants was learnt from his mother but, as often happens, he didn't fully appreciate the richness and variety of his own country's flora until he went to Germany as a young man. He describes his excitement on discovering Brazilian plants in the greenhouses of the botanical garden of Dahlem in Berlin. On returning home, he enrolled at the National School of Fine Arts in Rio; his professor, architect and town planner Lucia Costa, recognized his talent and gave him his first job.

Brazil was not generally known for its gardening culture and design, nor for the richness and variety of its native plants. In contrast to his contemporaries, who were busy importing foreign plants to use in their gardens, Burle Marx made many expeditions into the wild areas of Brazil to find and research species which might be suitable for cultivation. His personal collection of native plants now represents one of the world's finest resources of rainforest species. As a result, bromeliads, orchids, anthurium and alocasia have now been entrusted to the Brazilian government to safeguard for the future.

INDIGENOUS
PLANTING

◆

RIO DE JANEIRO,
BRAZIL

ROBERTO
BURLE MARX

Roberto Burle Marx's home is at Sitio, at the foot of a tropical, hilly Brazilian forest. When he began gardening, he didn't really appreciate the wonderful indigenous bromeliads; now, not only are they at home in his own garden, but he has shown Brazilians how to use them in theirs.

The use of native wild plants in his planting schemes put Burle Marx at the forefront of Brazilian garden design. The sight in gardens of what had been regarded as useless jungle vegetation came as a shock to many. Native plants became the hallmark of his designs, particularly his use of indigenous foliage, a rich diversity of leaf shape and colour planted in bold separate blocks, which is immediately recognizable as his work. He sometimes incorporated stones to separate the contrasting foliage varieties.

Burle Marx's gardens are never fussy; he felt that 'a garden has to have clarity to be understood and it must be understood to be enjoyed'. This well explains his predilection for simplicity of statement and boldness of design achieved by architectural foliage planting. Although his numerous artistic talents – as a designer of ceramics and textiles, as a painter and sculptor – contributed to his garden designs, at heart he was a botanist.

Metallic, painted cylindrical sculptures are the centrepieces of the sunken lawn with terraced gardens in front of the house, mostly planted with bromeliads.

INSCRIBED
IN STONE

◆

LITTLE SPARTA
LANARKSHIRE,
SCOTLAND

IAN
HAMILTON FINLAY

A tomb-like sculpture, slightly reminiscent of Aztec architecture, is surrounded by luxuriant foliage. The works are designed by Hamilton Finlay and commissioned from sculptors or masons.

IAN HAMILTON FINLAY was a prominent figure in the avant-garde movement of the 1960s which aimed at astonishing and, if possible, upsetting the bourgeois world. His book of poems, each consisting of one word, was a fair try. So, too, is his garden at Dunsyre in Lanarkshire. It is generally described as a poet's garden and has had some influence on young designers searching for the new, the unexpected and the faintly disturbing. Hamilton Finlay achieved such aims by means of surprising quotations in Greek or Latin carved on stone slabs, juxtaposed with classical columns, the whole dominated by a pair of garden temples, one of which consists of a homage to the leaders of the French Revolution.

We move into the twenty-first century with a cohort of young garden designers, some of whom have not yet shaken off the influence of this creative but puzzling personality, who exhibits in his garden a watering-can draped with a red sash and a tricolour rosette. And there is a fountain replica of an aircraft carrier. Has all this very much to do with the art of gardening?

Opposite A golden head, influenced by Roman art, rests in an uncultivated, wooded area. Roman inspiration is strong throughout the garden.

Above A pyramid constructed of grey stone is meant to have mystical significance, positioned amongst the trees which are left to grow wild in the garden.

Left Hamilton Finlay is fond of leaving messages – often perplexing ones – on the sculptures he commissions for his garden. Here the surrounding ground is not yet fully planted.

HIC
PERIERVNT AKAGI
KAGA SORYV HIRYV YORK-
TOWN AEQVORIS ALVI MELSVM
FLAMMIFERVM EA CONSVMPSIT
VNACVM EXAMINIBVS OPTIMIS
BATTLE OF MIDWAY 4 JUNE 1942
HERE PERISHED AKAGI KAGA SORYV
HIRYU YORKTOWN THE SEA-HIVES
CONSUMED WITH THEIR MOST
CHOICE SWARMS BY THEIR
OWN FLAME-BEARING
HONEY

A WOODLAND FLUTE

BETULA
PENDULA
CARPINUS
BETULUS
VIBURNUM
OPULUS
POPULUS
TREMULA
PRUNUS

Silver Birch, Hornbeam
Guelder Rose, Aspen, Plum

Above In a small clearing, another gnomic message, elegantly inscribed on black stone supported by turf and paving stones, confronts visitors.

Below A mysterious view over open countryside is visible from the edge of the garden. The top of an abstract sculpture emerges from bushes on the left of the lake.

Right A large, grey, inscribed stone is given a little grassed clearing amongst wild flowers and grasses.

Left A mixture of styles is evident in this pair of brick columns surmounted by stone carvings – half urn, half grenade – set unexpectedly amid trees and shrubs.

CHAPTER FIVE

GRASSES GALORE

MANY CONSIDER THEM WEEDS; some use them to fill gaps in floral arrangements; and in gardens they are often tolerated only in a few discreet clumps. But now grasses – varieties such as *Miscanthus, Festuca, Cortaderia* and *Molinia*, to name a few – are playing a leading role in many fashionable gardens as their design potential and beauty when domesticated are acknowledged.

In the past, we have tended to ignore the great variety of grasses that there is to choose from, in spite of the fact that we increasingly suffer from the poor soil conditions or cold winters that grasses are able to tolerate. Of all the available low-maintenance plants, grasses are the most versatile: they are not thirsty, they can be unobtrusive or impressive, and nearly all whisper in the wind.

Right The stems of bamboo are as decorative as they are sturdy and are frequently used for building, irrigation and decoration. Mature, established plants can grow as much as two metres a year.

Opposite In the Baruch Garden in Belgium (see page 194), clumps of grasses are planted like border shrubs, their graceful, arching wands contrasting with the clipped topiary in the background.

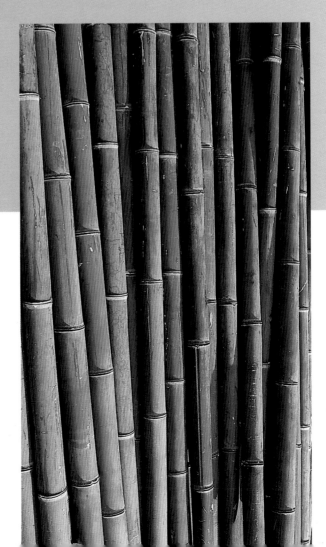

GRASSES GO DUTCH

◆

ARNHEM, NETHERLANDS

PIET OUDOLF

THE DUTCH GARDEN DESIGNER and nurseryman Piet Oudolf is one of the leading proponents of grasses. In his garden in the Netherlands, near Arnhem, Piet experiments with grasses, incorporating them in borders in dramatic ornamental groups. Unlike most plants, grasses have something to offer all year round. They emerge as graceful silhouettes as the seasons unfold, rustling in the spring breeze, stately and bold in the summer, shimmering, ghost-like under the winter frost. However overpowering some of the grasses may be, Piet does not try to control them by staking; rather, they stand grand and stately, erupting like fountains among a few chosen perennials, such as three-metre-tall *Aconitum episcopale* (my own never surpass two metres), recently introduced from China, rusty red achillea and *Thalictrum delavayi* 'Hewitt's Double', each rising over two metres tall. When these perennials retire under pressure of the cold, the grasses remain, threading their way through the borders. Ground-cover grasses are used in clumps of silver bristles which always look sprightly, as just before spring a certain amount of cutting back allows a fresh crop to grow through.

Left Piet Oudolf creates a rich
grass border of *Angelica
gigas*, *Miscanthus sinensis*
'Flamingo', *Persicaria
amplexicaulis* 'Rosea',
Centaurea 'Pulchra Major'
and *Calamagrostis
brachytricha*.

Right This is a perfect
demonstration of how
herbaceous plants marry well
with the various grasses in the
garden. The border
composition is of *Persicaria
amplexicaulis* 'Firetail',
Monarda didyma 'Fishes',
Centaurea 'Pulchra Major',
Echinops ritro 'Veitch's Blue',
Helenium 'Flammendes
Kätchen' and eupatorium.

Above Stipa offneri and *Eryngium decaisneanum* are happy in a dry gravel area where the drainage is maximized. *Left* Muted colours are displayed in swathes of monarda and *Achillea Filipendula* 'Parker's Variety'.

Previous pages Deschampsia goldschleiere, the billowing tufted annual grass, shows off pockets of *Trifolium repens*, *Digitalis ferruginea*, and *Verbascum x hybridum*.

To maximize the effect of the grasses, Piet and his wife, Anja, have planted evergreen background hedges against which the colour and structure of the plumes and reeds show up dramatically. Wherever you look in Piet's garden, it never looks bedraggled. The lack of flowers in this garden does not leave it colourless: the stems or stalks of the grasses are of yellow, brown, green, silver or variegated mixes. What is more, they knit together so closely that weeds don't have a chance to grow. Contrary to gardening gossip, grasses are not, in fact, invasive, apart from a couple of trouble-makers, *Glyceria* and *Phalaris*.

Apparently, it was the structure of grasses which first persuaded him to use them in his garden in such a determined fashion. Unlike most architectural plants, grasses are graceful, and the taller they are the more graceful still – even on a dull day when shrubs and perennials can look dowdy. With grasses, there is always a shimmer of light or a rustling movement among the plumes and seed heads. Piet Oudolf hasn't restricted his selection to ornamental border planting, but has been grass hunting diligently, discovering waterside grasses, dry area and wind-tolerant varieties. And the overriding beauty of grasses for a gardener (and I am looking out of the window at mine) is that they live frugally and die gracefully – quite an achievement.

The main grass used here is *Stipa offneri*, a good foil for the more colourful groups of *Salvia officinalis*, eryngium and lavender encroaching on the gravel.

91

MOUNTAIN GRASSES

◆

NEW SOUTH WALES, AUSTRALIA

MICHAEL COOKE

MICHAEL COOKE, GARDEN DESIGNER and nurseryman, has concentrated on using all the grass varieties of his central, mangrove home overlooking the Blue Mountains in Australia. In his garden, it is exciting to see the perennials we all know so well in such unusual company. The lush, dramatic forms of the native grasses complement the roses and the daring pink salvias and golden coreopsis, and when the flowers have finished their act, swaying autumn grasses create a new scene.

Michael and his wife Cathy lead a full double life, one half devoted to training horses, the other half to training Australians to experiment with the plants they produce for their nursery. The link between these two apparently disparate activities is the manure the horses produce for the plants cultivated in Michael's garden, which are then potted up for sale in the nursery.

Above A grass border is highlighted during summer and autumn with the bright pink heads of *Sedum spectabile*.

Left Kniphofia and grasses mingle well, especially for full summer effect. *Right Miscanthus sinensis* 'Zebrinus', sedum and evergreen, pointed-leaf phormium provide colour well into autumn.

92

CONIFERS AND GRASSES

◆

FOGGY BOTTOM NORFOLK, ENGLAND

ADRIAN BLOOM

The best way to ensure that grasses stand out is to give them a backing of dark evergreen such as the conifers pictured here. The group of plants in the centre consists of *Pinus heldreichii*, *Picea pungens* and *Juniperus chinensis* 'Aurea'. In the left-hand corner, the curving branches of *Juniperus communis* 'Oblonga Pendula' contribute to the backdrop for the ochre wands and metallic tufts of the grasses.

Grass and conifer borders surround the lawn – pinus and picea on the left behind low growing *Juniperus communis* 'Lakeland Silver' and *Pinus nigra* 'Hornibrookiana', foils for the varieties of miscanthus.

THIS GARDEN IS AN ATTACK on the prevailing gardening prejudice against conifers and on the lack of imagination usually shown in the planting of grasses. In his garden at Foggy Bottom in Norfolk, Adrian Bloom has created the perfect marriage between these two excitingly contrasting plants. The conifers provide the structure, what appears to be the masculine theme, of the garden, whilst the various coloured grasses seem to represent its feminine side, their appeal extending right through the year as they change colour, spread and become graceful. Adrian is not against including perennials in his garden, but warns that their planting must not be too tightly packed, as these less dominant plants will turn brown and soggy when pitted against the conifers and grasses. In any case, it is important that the conifers are permitted to show their silhouettes and that the grasses are allowed to spread. Adrian's garden is really a demonstration of the modern version of the herbaceous border – except that it contains grasses instead.

THE GARDEN OF MANOR FARMHOUSE in Patney, England, is a good example of how a visual impact can be achieved with only two major features, here a grass mound and a meadow. The landscape designer Michael Balston adopted this modern, labour-saving gardening option firstly because he had a pile of rubble to dispose of and, secondly, because such a garden would be fun for children. Once the rubble had been piled up, topsoil was carpeted over it to create the mound. The planting of grasses in spiral form allowed for an ascending footpath to the top of the mound. This living pyramid is situated in a flowering meadow, through which a grass path is cut by lawnmower.

The mound becomes the background scenery of the garden and the meadow its foreground. The meadow then provides a continuous seasonal flower show, starting with snowdrops, moving on to *Crocus tommasinianus*, then *Narcissus lobularis*, followed by a succession of daffodils, until the end of April. During spring, large areas of fritillaries and then bluebells (mostly Spanish) also flower; in May, camassia, together with *Narcissus poeticus*, old pheasant eye and clouds of cow parsley take over. About this time, the grasses also start to come into their own, with species like meadow foxtail, false broom, cock's foot, bent and fescue. In June and early July, the meadow is thick with buttercups and ox-eye daisies. Fun, easy-going and unpretentious, I feel sure this garden will be an inspiration to many people.

The mound is both futuristic and accommodating, set amongst spring-flowering trees and bulbs.

EXCLUSIVELY BAMBOO

◆

BAMBOUSERAIE
ANDUZE, FRANCE

YVES & MURIEL CROUZET

Right Originally from China, then cultivated in Japan and India, later arriving in Europe, the phyllostachys grows over twenty metres tall to form a green, vaulted, cathedral-like archway.

Below Culms of *Phyllostachys edulis pubescens*, native to China, the shoots of which are an edible delicacy. A shoot can grow one metre in twenty-four hours.

THE RICHNESS AND DIVERSITY OF the exotic planting at La Bambouseraie in Prafrance tends to disguise the fact that it is essentially a bamboo garden. A few years ago, bamboo was considered exotic and not adaptable to Western climates and was hardly ever used. Perhaps, too, it was difficult to visualize in our traditional perennial, shrubby gardens. But now our gardening projects are not always concerned simply with design and style, but may emphasize instead the plants themselves, and bamboo is certainly the dominant idea of the garden in Prafrance.

The Bambouseraie had a tumultuous birth in 1855 when Eugene Mazel, who had made a fortune importing spices from Asia, decided to buy thirty-four hectares of land to make a garden. Mazel's passion was botany and his travels and shipping activities enabled him to import many exotic plants to Prafrance to fulfil his dream, the creation of a 'bambouseraie'. The word didn't exist until Mazel thought it up, as bamboo was rarely seen on this side of the world.

To establish his exotic garden, Mazel needed prodigious quantities of water, because bamboo is a notoriously thirsty plant. He undertook a vast project to drain water from the nearby river. Large numbers of exotic plants arrived in Mazel's ships and a dozen gardeners were brought onto the site, but Mazel's dream collapsed for lack of funds. In 1890, he was ruined and had to abandon the Bambouseraie to his creditors. But the dream found another chance of realization when the garden was bought in 1902 by Gaston Negre, who pledged to save the remains of the collection of bamboo and exotic plants. Now another generation, Gaston Negre's granddaughter, Muriel, and her husband, Yves Crouzet, have taken over the site, determined to enrich and develop the Bambouseraie by introducing new and exotic varieties of bamboo and by exploring the numerous uses for this wonderful plant.

We in the West are just beginning to discover the diversity of bamboo, which has been cultivated for thousands of years in China and Japan. Most people view bamboo as a plant suited to hot climates alone, although some varieties are, in fact, perfectly acclimatized to cold winters. They can die from lack of water, but not from cold. This could explain why the mulching of young shoots is of great importance. When exposed to severe cold, the leaves will suffer first. If the buds remain undamaged, culms grow green again as soon as the temperature rises; if they are damaged, the culms fade and die. But if the rhizomes themselves have not suffered, they will grow new shoots in the following spring.

In Europe, bamboo has been used sparingly by garden designers, except in their more avant-garde projects. One of the main reasons for its restricted use in the West may be

Lysichitons are beginning to colonize the nymphaea pond, along with clumps of *Chimonobambusa marmorea*, whose stems turn red in autumn.

that we find colour so important. But green is a colour, and so is yellow. The long and graceful leaves of bamboo can be of all manner of colour tones – variegated green and white, gold and green – and the stems attractive blacks, browns or greens.

Today we know much more about bamboo and its hundreds of varieties and many uses in the garden, to the extent that almost every garden problem can be solved by the introduction of bamboo. The bamboo *Pleioblastus* can be used to establish lawns; *Sasa masmuneana* can form topiary; a forest reaching twelve or fifteen metres high can be established with the graceful *Phyllostachys bambusoides;* and a green or golden hedge can be planted with *Sasa tsuboiana*. All these varieties are compact and dense enough to discourage weeds, or even to keep out rabbits. Bamboo windbreaks are also very effective and, just to show how versatile bamboo really is, Muriel and Yves Crouzet have recently created a bamboo maze with *Sinarundinaria*!

The growing of bamboo for food, a tradition in Asia, is now developing around the world. Bamboo sprouts fresh out of the ground are prepared and eaten in many different ways. Bamboo holds the plant record for rapid growth: it takes a culm approximately two months to grow and young shoots growing one metre within twenty-four hours are no rarity. A patient observer may even watch them grow as he would watch the hour-hand of a clock. In fact, one day I watched my friend Sir Peter Smithers, a great bamboo enthusiast, crouched beside a clump of bamboo in his garden, knife in hand, as the head of the sprouting bamboo emerged before our eyes. He snipped it off for lunch and it tasted really delicious, very similar to asparagus.

Above The tallest bamboos, some reaching over twenty metres, can form big clumps of impenetrable forest. *Below* The stream running through the Bambouseraie's Japanese garden is planted with deciduous trees and bamboo.

Left Sasaella masamuneana albostriata, a hardy bamboo which stands only twenty centimetres tall, is a compact, dwarf variety which spreads rapidly and can be used as a topiary feature or as ground cover in damp woodland.

In Japan, you will not find a single garden without bamboo, either as a vegetable, as fencing, formed into a pergola or in the shape called 'lion's tooth', where a piece of bamboo is balanced on a horizontal axle. As one end of the bamboo fills with rainwater, it makes the whole thing tip over and empty; as it swings back to its original position, it hits a stone, making a noise which is said to be capable of frightening a lion (if a lion happens to pass by). A more pleasing sound is that made by various lengths of bamboo canes suspended on wires to create musical notes when strummed.

The same diversity of uses for bamboo is seen in China, as Colonel Barrington de Fontblanque describes: 'What would a poor Chinese do without bamboo? Aside from the fact that it gives him his food, he uses it to make the roof of his house, the bed he sleeps in, the cup he drinks from and the spoon he eats with. He waters his field with bamboo tubes, his crops are harvested with a rake made of bamboo, the grain is winnowed with a bamboo basket. The mast of his boat, as well as the handles of his barrow, are made of bamboo. He is beaten with a bamboo cane, tortured by bamboo points and finally, the rope that strangles him also is made of bamboo.'

A bamboo with short narrow sheaths and papery white margins makes a good evergreen ground cover.

Let's hope that some of the employments of bamboo have changed since Fontblanque's days. Contemporary uses include the reinforcement of concrete with weathered bamboo and using its pulp to make paper. The latter might contribute in some way to the preservation of endangered forests, which have taken hundreds of years to establish. Bamboo, by contrast, can be felled and re-established in the space of only a few years.

I always think of a garden as an outdoor house where not only vegetation, but artwork, fences, gazebos, bridges, pergolas, trellis and furniture have their role to play. All these decorative additions can be made out of bamboo and have the advantage of being weatherproof. What other plant lends itself to such a variety of uses?

CHAPTER SIX

FORWARD TO THE PAST

COULD IT BE NOSTALGIA? Could it be the need to recapture security in a world where violence and uncertainty predominate? Or is recreating a familiar environment in the garden a form of regression, a harking back to our childhoods? Perhaps the trend is little different from the fantasy world in which Marie Antoinette played out the role of a simple dairy maid in her make-believe farm at Versailles, a game which must have given the Queen of France a sense of safety lacking in her everyday life.

The past, for many, is idealized as the good old days, an era which can be reinvented today. We have our museums to ensure that nothing of the past of the fine and decorative arts is lost, and some of our gardener designers, thankfully, have the same approach to gardening.

Below At Heligan in Cornwall, the original path has been restored around an ancient well-head which was once buried under tons of earth and vegetation. This mossy, man-made rock mound, together with fern trees and rhododendrons, has immediately taken over and the plants prosper in the newly discovered light.

Opposite The jungle bog garden is an ideal habitat for yellow flowering lysichitons and giant leaf *Gunnera manicata* whose brownish, pinnate flowers can be seen in the background. Its dried leaves will protect the crown of the plant from winter frosts.

103

A MEDIEVAL
DREAM

◆

ABBAYE D'ORSAN
BERRY, FRANCE

SONIA LESOT &
PATRICE TARAVELLA

I N THE HEART OF THE BERRY DISTRICT of France, Notre Dame d'Orsan is celebrating the restoration of its nine-hundred-year-old Priory gardens. In 1992, two young architects, Sonia Lesot and Patrice Taravella, began to restore the potagers, vines, orchards, arbours, cloister and enclosures of the property, where a twelfth-century religious community once lived in complete autarchy. Orsan was founded by Robert d'Arbrissel, one of the most prestigious predicators and controversial ascetics of the church of his day, who claimed that to experience carnal temptations was the best way to surmount them. He bequeathed his heart to be buried in the Priory cemetery and its miraculous properties were held to be responsible for an even greater expansion of Orsan's community.

Sonia and Patrice were faced with the dilemma of whether they should respect all the historical details of the Priory and restore it accordingly, or whether the restoration could employ modern techniques and equipment. They decided to be guided by documents relating to the Priory and by miniature medieval paintings, but not to be restricted by them. The important thing was to re-create the spirit of the place. After all, if the garden's primary function had been to feed the body, its other role was to provide food for thought, and it seemed legitimate to continue in such a tradition.

Gilles Guillet joined the team as gardener in order to solve the botanical problems posed by Orsan and to give the project horticultural credibility. Fortunately, plants growing elsewhere in the region provided the key to the numerous varieties of fruits, vegetables and even flowers which were probably once cultivated in the Priory gardens. The three main purposes of a monastery garden were that it be functional, symbolic and aesthetic. The functional gardens were devoted to edible plants such as vegetables, herbs and fruits. Plaited, chestnut-edged raised beds called *plessis*, which afforded the easy gathering of herbs and vegetables, were re-created at Orsan using twelfth-century illuminated

The general plan of a religious community such as Orsan is evident in this aerial view, showing how buildings were designed to enclose the priory grounds and geometric plots laid out to separate the various functions of the garden.

Above Raised beds created
by weaving branches of
chestnuts are filled with straw
to keep vegetables warm.
These *plessis* were also used
for planting herbs.

Right In the raised beds,
pumpkins (pictured here),
onions, cucumbers, gourds
and marrows are easy to
maintain as they ripen
in the sun.

A pergola of rustic birch divides the garden in two, separating the vegetable area from the rose garden. Plum trees are being trained in the way in which they might have been in medieval times.

manuscripts as inspiration. The *plessis,* in fact, originally had many uses: as fencing, as animal enclosures, or as feeding troughs. Much time and thought was given to the techniques used for their reconstruction at Orsan so that they would last well and be in keeping with a medieval design.

After consulting archaeologists and historians, Sonia and Patrice realized that they had very little reliable information about the precise species of plants grown by such religious communities, as the monasteries were all destroyed during the French Revolution. However, the general plan of a medieval garden was more or less universal and well documented elsewhere in Europe. Herbs, vines and, when the climate permitted, trees were always grown. The restoration of Orsan's gardens doesn't pretend to be an exact replica of monastery planting in the twelfth century, but it does contain a variety of the plants and features that the monks would certainly have cultivated. 'We feel sure,' says Guillet by way of example, 'that in the centre of the cloister there would have been a fountain. Many illuminated texts tend to confirm this; therefore we built a simple water feature where we knew it would have existed in a medieval garden.' This is the symbolic aspect of the garden: the four axes of the world meet around a fountain representing the four rivers of earthly paradise – Phison, Geon, Tiger and Euphrates. The cloister is also

adorned with vines, roses, lavender and jasmine, and it was a place where prayers were said and where meditations reflected on the promised Paradise.

In the rose and flower garden, which fulfilled the aesthetic function of the design, the monks would nevertheless not have been particularly concerned to create a pleasing floral display. Flowers would more likely have been chosen for their perfume, for apothecary uses, or as offerings to the Virgin Mary, who enjoyed a high status in such communities. Nevertheless, Sonia Lesot and Patrice Taravella felt that the spirit of Orsan would not be compromised if the gardens of today were to offer a selection of beautiful perfumed plants. There was also once a herbarium devoted to medicinal plants, most of which could be found in local fields and ditches. A cemetery was laid out under the fruit trees and a secret garden with arbours and seats contained flowers to decorate the chapel.

The importance of its gardens to a religious community is perhaps surprising, but it is worth remembering that an abbey such as Orsan housed possibly twenty or more brothers who needed to be entirely self-sufficient. Gardening and baking, cooking and distilling wine were major tasks to be performed, second only to praying and meditating. The restoration of the gardens at Orsan is an important step in our understanding of the way of life of a such a medieval community.

Above and below Throughout the rose garden, rustic wooden pergolas, avenues and tripods are designed to accommodate climbing varieties.

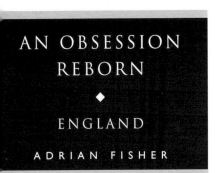

AN OBSESSION REBORN

◆

ENGLAND

ADRIAN FISHER

MAZES AND LABYRINTHS originated some five thousand years ago in Ancient Egypt, which begs the question why they feature in a book about twenty-first-century gardening. The answer lies in the current growing enthusiasm for new and more and more ingenious mazes. No one is more enthusiastic – euphoric even – than Adrian Fisher, designer and builder of mazes all over Europe, the Americas and the Far East. Fisher has been designing mazes since 1975 and many of his creations will reach their full maturity in the early years of the twenty-first century.

Mazes, traditional and new, are to be found in the gardens of the great palaces and country houses of Britain – Blenheim Palace, Hatfield House, Hampton Court, Hever and Leeds Castles and dozens more. At Longleat House, the Marquis of Bath has five mazes and is always building more. Meanwhile, in the USA, the 'maize maze' is growing in popularity. These huge structures cut paths through fields of growing maize and achieve world records for length. Designed by Adrian Fisher and his collaborator, Don Frantz, they are very American entertainments, with background music and 'maze masters' in towers to offer hope and encouragement to anyone lost and panicking along the miles of paths. When the corn is harvested at summer's end, the maze simply disappears.

Adrian Fisher tells me he has some thirty maze projects at any one time on his drawing-board at his home in southern England. Some are permanent hedge or brick mazes in

This paving maze in the courtyard of Kentwell Hall in Suffolk, England, was designed and built in 1985 by Adrian Fisher. It consists of 27,000 clay paving bricks laid out in the shape of a Tudor Rose to celebrate the 500th anniversary of the Tudor royal dynasty.

public or private gardens; some are temporary maize mazes in fields of growing corn; some are vast and designed to give anyone venturing into them a three-kilometre walk; and some are intimate and purely decorative. 'Mazes are really about fun. They are a focus in the garden for the whole family to enjoy themselves, play hide and seek, get lost, get grandparents playing with their grandchildren,' says Adrian Fisher.

As a Liveryman of the Worshipful Company of Gardeners of London, Fisher sees mazes with a gardener's eye. 'Over the centuries they have had deep mystical and religious significance. We find them in the form of labyrinths in cathedrals, on sites of ancient worship and even reproduced on early tombstones, on Etruscan vases and in sacred texts.'

Today, we could see mazes as metaphors for the uncertainties and false starts of human life, leading in the end to some kind of paradise, or perhaps not. More likely we now just see them as fun and attractive features. They are certainly not beyond the resources or the space of a modest garden. They can be designed as a pattern in brick or paving stones on the surface of a patio, or as an outline in stones, low box, turf, fragrant low-growing plants, or even bent willow, at a suitable spot in the garden. A maze will be especially popular with the family children and their friends – and it will help to keep them off the flower beds, too!

Opposite above 'Veronica's maze' at Parham Park in southern England was inspired by an embroidered coverlet from the house. The maze is based on a curling brick path laid in grass and is contemporary in appearance.

A WATER
MAZE

◆

HEVER CASTLE
KENT, ENGLAND

THIS UNIQUE WATER-SPLASHING MAZE at Hever Castle is situated on a sixteen-acre island set between the River Eden and the lake. The maze and its integral folly together form an exciting circular garden feature.

Proceeding on stepping stones, the water maze challenges you to reach a central folly within the pond, whilst avoiding various water features. The stepping-stone paths may lead to various water obstacles, formed by jets of water, making you divert to find an alternative, drier way to the centre. The maze stepping stones have been planted with 14,000 baskets of aquatic plants. The outside of the folly itself is awash with cascades of water, and inside a special water feature has a spiral staircase leading to the top for an elevated view of the maze and across to the lake and Italian Gardens.

Y OWN FAVOURITE GROTTO is the marvellous creation of Isaac de Caus at Woburn Abbey. He built it for the 4th Duke of Bedford in about 1630 and it is the oldest surviving grotto in Britain. It is really a room within the abbey with access through a couple of doorways to the garden, rather than a garden feature. But it is a fairyland, encrusted with thousands of shells arranged in intriguing patterns, including dolphins, mermaids and assorted sea gods – a deeply satisfying folly.

I have never quite decided whether the charm of a grotto lies in sitting snug inside and gazing out at a landscape by Repton, Brown or Le Notre, or coming upon one at the end of an avenue of birches or azaleas. They make slightly weird and exotic statements in the rococo style, reminiscent of an entirely imaginary age of excess, eccentricity and aristocratic ease, long since past.

The history of grottoes stretches back into Greek and Roman antiquity. Their heyday in France was in the sixteenth century – for example, at the chateau of the Bastie d'Urfe (1551) and at Versailles, where the famous Grotto of Thetis was destroyed in 1684 when

A shell grotto arbour in a London town house was built in 1997–8 by Belinda Eade to enliven a small, paved rear garden.

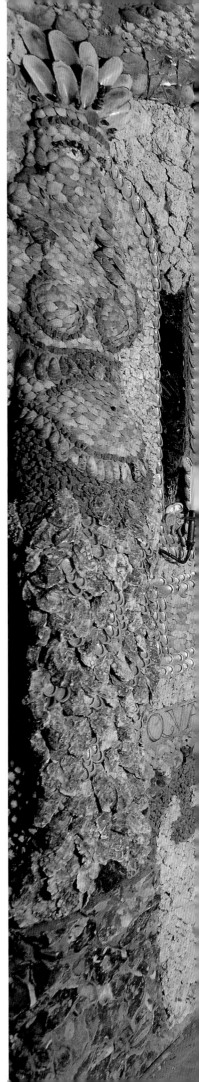

Grottoes are usually designed as caves, but this unusual new version is built as an antechamber walk through to the garden of a London house.

The decoration is mainly shells with tufa borders, with knapped flint on the lower wall surfaces. The floor consists of a mosaic of marble rectangles laid as a labyrinth.

Right An eye-catcher at the end of a town garden. The statue stands in front of a grotto backdrop of mussel shells and tufa. The effect is romantic, mysterious and intriguing.

Above A cartouche of the head of Bacchus is mounted on a wall in a London garden. The technique is typical of the decoration of grottoes using sea shells from different continents.

Mansart built the north wing of the chateau. In England, they came into vogue in the eighteenth century, when the collecting of seashore shells became a respectable pastime for aristocratic young ladies with little skill and endless time on their hands. Wonderful examples can still be seen at Leeds Castle, Goldney Hall, Painshill Park and at Stourhead. The shells, and other bric-a-brac such as glass fragments, shards of china, feldspar – almost anything which could be found and easily transported – were meticulously fastened to the walls of small stone buildings, which were then decorated with classical statuary.

Today, a small number of talented practitioners are reviving the art of the grotto, creating new ones or refurbishing some of the many survivors from the past. The English sculptor Belinda Eade has restored and created grottoes in England, Greece and the USA. She detects a marked increase in interest in grottoes, even in thoroughly unconventional locations well away from the grand landscapes that housed them in earlier centuries. This new enthusiasm may be part of a nostalgia for a mythical past, a feature of the malaise of our *fin-de-siècle*. A grotto can add charm and interest in a large or even in a medium-sized garden, and its creation can while away many hours in harmless fun, searching for pretty shells on the beach (though the shells will take a lot of cleaning if you don't want your grotto to smell like a fish market!), or even in the breaking up of disused crockery with a hammer.

Belinda Eade recommends plastering the interior of the grotto, twenty centimetres at a time, with lime mortar for an old building, or with sand and cement for a newer one. Then push in the shells, stones or other oddments. Your own grotto could bear the date 2000 and you could build it in the back garden of your town house. Why not?

MARGOT KNOX is a renowned Australian artist and a competent gardener who has put her craftsmanship to use in an original and very personal way by 'tiling' her garden. When she first acquired the property, it was a most uninviting prospect, a redundant, red-brick church hall on a busy road. Unexpectedly, a eucalyptus and a rotary clothes line were its only attributes. Undaunted, Margot says she was delighted to have to tackle so many constraints. The eucalyptus indicated at least that something *could* live.

A few decades ago, a railway employee in Chartres, known as Monsieur Pique Assiette, covered his house and every piece of furniture in it with broken crockery. A similar approach, but one involving a finer artistic sense, has inspired Margot Knox to ornament her garden with cut tiles, thereby reviving and modernizing an ancient mosaic art, vestiges of which have been found on archaeological sites around the Mediterranean. It all started four years ago, when she wanted a sculptured sofa, rather than a garden bench. Her son, designer Alexander Knox, built the sofa from bricks, steel and concrete, and Margot set about upholstering it in tiles with lovely glowing greens, energizing blues, warm orange and red dashes.

She used Monsieur Pique Assiette's well-proven method of construction, which runs as follows. Work out a design on squared paper, then scale it up and mark it onto the area to be covered using chalk, charcoal or wax. Then cut the tiles to shape using specialist tile clippers (repeating shapes give more coherence than randomly broken tiles). Then, either 'butter' each piece with cement and put into place, or cement an area and press the pieces

Part of the garden shows Knox's unique use of plants combined with mosaic tiles to create exotic background pictures, here decorating a low wall and the entrance to a little garden room.

into it (work on small areas at a time or the cement will begin to set before the pieces are in place). Gaps must be left between the pieces for grout. When the cement has set completely (allow at least twenty-four hours) fill the cracks with tilers' grouting mixture. Remove any excess grout before it sets with a damp cloth. Once dry (another twenty-four hours), polish the tiles with a dry cloth. Bear in mind, says Margot, the effects of weather and climate, especially if they might induce expansion and contraction. Mosaics cannot be totally sealed and if water trapped into the mosaic freezes, the tiles may crack. In the UK, frost can also lift the glaze from normal ceramic tiles; specialist mosaic tiles, which have the colour fired in, are preferable.

To add volume to the narrow strips of garden, Margot has created emerging boulders, like weighty stone sculptures, of cement and bricks, held in shape with chicken wire. They are then adorned with a moulding of vibrant, jewel-like mosaic. Margot says that her boulders are reminiscent of the Australian landscape, except that the rough, weathered surfaces have given way to ones of colour and fun – a fallen star, a patch of grass, a butterfly, a radiant flower, a beetle. The path walks have been roughly gravelled, inlaid with crazy-paving slabs of mosaic at random. Amid a planting of arum lilies and grasses, a small water feature bubbles away in its mosaic pond. The largest canvas on which Margot has worked is the walls of the house, where the colours are more subdued, like a patchwork of various stones. Here and there she got carried away and added a second layer of cut tiles in the shape of floating flowers.

Margot Knox's dramatic garden sofa was built by her son in brick, steel and concrete which she then decorated in vividly coloured tiles. The result is much more intriguing than an ordinary garden bench.

A giant container pot has been lavishly decorated with an exotic design worked in coloured tiles – an ideal home for an equally exotic plant.

A mosaic tablet naming the garden is made from broken pieces of blue-and-white tableware.

All around the garden, huge mosaic urns, extraordinarily vibrant in their design and colour, are planted with bold leaf shrubs which have an air of exotic patio plants. Margot Knox is particularly interested in strong, architectural planting, achieved with single specimens and by planting in large groups. The structure of the plants is more important than their colour. As a result, she has chosen Abyssinian bananas, masses of agave, aloe, loquats, giant white strelitzia, echium and dianella, with their strappy green leaves and lapis lazuli berries.

'Maybe it's kitsch, maybe it's over the top,' says Margot, but there is more artistic thought to it than at first meets the eye. Her talent as a gardener has turned what could have been kitsch into a genuinely artistic achievement. It would be hard to say whether the plants were chosen to harmonize with the mosaic or whether the mosaic was designed to enhance the planting; the symbiotic relationship between the two creates a new artistry. What started as an embellishment to her home and as a hobby has now become an enjoyable career.

A BOTANICAL GARDEN

◆

LA GARDE ADHEMAR, FRANCE

DANIELLE ARCUCCI

LA GARDE ADHEMAR, a forgotten mountain village in the Rhone Valley, has suddenly appeared on the tourist map. Built into the mountain side, the village and its old Romanesque church overlook the setting sun, behind the powerful nuclear station of Pierrelatte. Here past and present have come to terms with each other through the creation of a unique garden. Danielle Arcucci, the deputy mayor of the village, galvanized the community into making a botanical herb garden on the disused terraces in front of the ancient ramparts. Coming out of church, after weddings, funerals or Sunday mass, the 'Lagardiens', as the villagers are called, were wont to lean over the parapet and look down on a wasteland of weeds and rubble where vegetables and crops were grown in days gone by. Danielle felt sure that something beautiful and instructive could be created on this derelict site. Her choice of a herb garden was inspired by the local valley flora, which boasts dozens of different herbs which are used for perfume, for dyeing and in medicine.

Daughter of Marius, the late head gardener of the famous Borelli Park in Marseille, Danielle was born into the gardening world. At La Garde Adhemar, she set out on her

project by drawing up a simple plan of action on naive, bold and symmetrical principles. Twelve borders were to illustrate the rays of the sun, and on a lower level, twenty-five borders to make a star design. The planting was a labour of love. Raymond Girbaud, the Mayor, his deputy and the entire council all turned their hands and knees to gardening.

The planting of 5500 edging box plants alone took nearly two years, along with the cuttings of herbs, which had to be sorted and identified. At the foot of each species, a coloured name plate indicates not only the name of the plant but also its medicinal use. For example, a dark yellow label indicates herbs used for liver disorders; a grey one for herbs for the intestinal tract; red for the cardiovascular system; and so on. Several hundred different herbs have been collected, including mint, lavender, thyme, madder, santolina, rare Mexican sage reaching two metres tall, twenty-eight varieties of geranium, artemesia, rosemary, thrift, salvia, arnica, rue, myrtle, balm, hyssop, angelica, not forgetting all the popular cooking herbs, such as the alliums. The local police turn a blind eye to the intoxicating poppy seed, quite illegal but so pretty, and I doubt that the children's botany lesson explains the ancient administration of *Agnus Castus* to monks to temper their sexual ardour.

Situated on the west side of the mountain, basking in the afternoon and setting sun, the plants are favourably exposed. Each variety has its special bed, as was once prescribed in medieval herb gardens to make herb picking by the nuns easier and safer. Raymond Girbaud is a good mason; Robert Boyer, a chemical engineer at the nuclear power station, handles barrows of manure; other councillors, several working at the power station, all chip in after work.

Every year, old plants are discarded and new varieties brought in. Nurseries throughout the country and some specialist nurseries in England contribute to the introduction of new varieties. The whole effect of the colourful herbs, as Miss Jekyll would put it, is of an 'optical gastronomy'. Many visitors now flock to La Garde Adhemar to see the garden. Entrance is free because, Danielle Arcucci says, it is a gift to those who enjoy it.

Above left Colourful beds of pansies were planted for their perfume, but were once used as laxatives. An infusion of pansies was also brewed to treat eczema. Pansy flowers can be eaten in salads, too.

Above right High on the old village walls above the garden, a ceramic plaque records its name.

Opposite The herbs are laid out in individual beds, each edged in box and symbolizing the rays of the sun. The pattern can be clearly appreciated from this viewing-point over the wall.

A SLEEPING BEAUTY

◆

HELIGAN CORNWALL, ENGLAND

TIM SMIT

Opposite A very rare wall of bee boles was rediscovered among the tree ferns after seventy years of neglect.

Below The majestic tree fern *Dicksonia antarctica* has flourished unrestrained since Victorian times, creating a dense canopy forest.

THERE IS REALLY NOTHING QUITE LIKE the Lost Gardens of Heligan, the brainchild of an immensely energetic and talented entrepreneur from the popular music industry. Tim Smit, together with his friend John Nelson, came across Heligan by chance in 1990. The place was a ruin, the result of seventy years of total neglect after the Tremayne family had thrown up their hands in horror at the crippling cost of maintaining some sixty acres of garden. 'Heligan,' says Tim Smit, 'is among the oldest gardens in Cornwall, with many of its plants predating the rush of the late nineteenth- and early twentieth-century introductions. Ironically, through neglect, it has retained most of the important plants in its collection, many of which have grown to a great size, cocooned in the overgrowth from which we rescued them. Our experience of discovery, unveiling the garden, was enhanced by a feeling of fellow-spiritedness with those who had brought the original plants back from their travels. Each exotic shrub or tree has an adventure attached to it and a story to tell. For sheer bravery, the great nineteenth- and early twentieth-century plant hunters are hard to beat.'

In Cornwall, gardens like Heligan have been dying at the rate of one every two years for the past fifty years or more. In the case of Heligan, a hundred and thirty years of expansion and new planting, since the eighteenth century, suddenly stopped. There was to be no replanting or modernizing, not even minimal maintenance. The place gently went to sleep. Now, under Smit's inspired guidance, it has been shaken awake, not as a development of the past, but as a loving refurbishment, complete with every archaic, obsolete technique and installation that the restorers can discover. We are now able to learn how, with cleverly handmade tools and great dedication, these lavish gardens were originally created.

One of the outstanding rhododendrons in the garden has grown into a giant tree over a period of several hundred years. Now that the gardens have been restored, it has acquired a new vigour.

In his book about the Lost Gardens of Heligan, Tim Smit dispels a myth perpetrated by modern garden writers, who 'have a tendency to see the past through rose-tinted glasses. The only roses in the Melon Garden were there to provide a screen for the path through it that led up to the pleasure grounds. The image of ladies in gingham dresses bearing Sussex trugs filled to bursting with cut flowers and vegetables that have never seen earth or insects is romantic hokum. The reality was that these working parts of the garden stank to high heaven! At Heligan, more than a dozen different types of manure were in regular use as a composting or heating medium, including what was euphemistically referred to as "human night-soil" – the slops from the cesspit next to the two-storey building, in addition to all the material coming up from the Big House. In his growing notes for prize chrysanthemums, the head gardener ascribed his success to the use of "seven-year-old goose shit". One assumes that it wasn't the age of the goose he was talking about . . .

'The other myth that needs dispelling is that the Victorians were dedicated to healthy, organic methods. In reality, gardeners in the nineteenth century were spraying sulphur, cyanide, nicotina and strychnine on almost anything. The staff who worked in the glasshouses didn't have high hopes of enjoying their retirement, and not for nothing did the brass sprayers earn the monicker "widow-makers".'

Above Giant rhododendrons at the water's edge of the top lake at Heligan are complemented by a fine display of water lilies. The lake was first mapped in 1770.

Right Restoration of the steep-sided, sub-tropical valley was started in 1992. Vegetation includes tree ferns, many bamboos and other species.

Above In Victorian times, the flower garden at Heligan grew varieties to be cut for the house. The glasshouses, which still survive, were used for exotic and tender plants and various fruits.

Right Pineapples were a delicacy in the great houses of the Victorian era. The pineapple pits at Heligan have been restored.

Amongst the restored areas of the gardens are the Victorian pineapple pits. What exactly is the point of reintroducing the obsolete craft of growing pineapples in the harsh northern climate of England? The answer is that at Heligan, the revival in all its historic complexity of a dead gardening tradition brings more visitors to remote Cornwall than to any other private garden in Britain. For Tim Smit has tapped into a vein of widespread nostalgia for a past way of life – a nostalgia which is unprecedented in gardening history. The garden as a museum has arrived, but there is nothing static about the venture. It will be a continual process, the past linked to the present.

There are many wonderful things to be seen at Heligan, as in any good museum: a beautiful Italian Garden; a New Zealand Garden; a Sundial Garden with perennial and herbaceous borders; a grotto; a mysterious ravine; and fabulous tree ferns. Heligan probably has the largest collection of tree ferns in Britain – primitive and beautiful relics from a time when dinosaurs walked the earth. They adapted well through the years of neglect and the only ones that have died appear to have had their tops rubbed out by the branches of invasive trees growing next to them.

Tim Smit says his aim has been to 'tell the story of the gardens from the point of view of the ordinary men and women whose sweat and blood created them.' Perhaps it is only in Britain, where a passion for gardening is matched by an equal passion for the past, that a mad but glorious venture like Heligan can be carried through to national acclaim.

This greenhouse in Heligan's flower garden was derelict when Tim Smit and his associates rescued Heligan in the last decade of the twentieth century.

CHAPTER SEVEN

MODERN SCULPTURE IN THE GARDEN

Sculptures have adorned gardens since they were first created, but as the twentieth century came to an end, gardeners everywhere began to bid farewell to the nymphs and dryads that traditionally lined avenues and punctuated vistas. In march the modernists in their place, the sculptors in modern materials, creators of challenging forms, purveyors of new and sometimes uncomfortable ideas. The sculpture they create is very much at home in the natural surroundings in which it is placed. It is not by chance that some of the most exciting designers who use sculpture in garden settings have worked in England, the recognized birthplace of the modern movement in sculpture.

Left 'The Two of Us', 1997–8, by Steven Gregory, bronze, three and a half metres high, one of an edition of three, in Hat Hill Copse, Sussex, England.

Details of sculptures by Sally Matthews. *Above right* 'Four Welsh Mountain Ponies' in felted wool, wood and steel frame at Gatwnant, South Wales. *Below right* 'Five Wolves' in cement, wood, steel and grass.

A WOODLAND
GALLERY

◆

HAT HILL COPSE
SUSSEX, ENGLAND

WILFRED &
JEANETTE CASS

HAT HILL COPSE, one of the world's finest sculpture gardens, is the unique achievement of Wilfred and Jeannette Cass. They have created this wonderful environment out of twenty acres of neglected woodland on the South Downs, and now exhibit as many as forty sculptures there at any one time. Each year, about twelve sculptures are changed, giving new young artists a chance to exhibit their work. This, combined with a carefully devised programme of new plantings in the woodland, ensures that Hat Hill Copse is constantly developing and moving forward.

The house at Hat Hill Copse, built in 1977 and designed on the Bauhaus principle of repeated cubes, struck the Casses as an ideal setting for their important collection of modern art. They moved here in 1989, starting to mould the overgrown and neglected woodland into an environment in which to display sculpture. Many trees had fallen in the fierce storm of 1987 and much of the site was a scene of devastation. Vines of old man's beard had to be cleared, fallen and dead trees hauled out and the woodland generally needed to be thinned out considerably. Walks and open spaces were cut out of the undergrowth to open up views southwards, across farmland, to the Roman city of

Above 'Trilobites', 1989, by Tony Cragg, a bronze two metres in height. The sculptor has found inspiration in marine fossils of the Palaeozoic era.

Right 'Secret Life', 1994' by Peter Randall Page, 1.57 metres in length. Part of a granite series in which the sculptor suggests that there is always more within a stone, or within ourselves, than at first appears.

Above 'Large Space Venus', 1986, by William Turnbull. Bronze with green patina on a York stone base, 1.87 metres in height. The piece combines the form of an utilitarian object with an elusive configuration.

Right 'Herd of Arches', 1994, by Andy Goldsworthy, sandstone and slate, approximately 15 metres in length. The sculpture is placed along a wooded pathway.

Chichester; the elegant eleventh-century cathedral spire can now be glimpsed at the end of cunningly planned vistas through the trees. Several hundred trees were specially planted, selected for their grace and for their autumn colour: aspen (*Populus tremula*) so called because of its dainty leaves that tremble in the wind; acers, with their flaming autumn leaves; many flowering hawthorns; Irish yew; and copper beeches.

Each sculpture has its forest environment carefully created in advance. The forestry work is virtually continuous, with many new trees planted annually, so it is possible to give each important piece a uniquely designed setting. Roughly half an acre of land is devoted to each individual piece. On the day I visited Hat Hill Copse, Wilfred Cass showed me the site which had been prepared for the imminent arrival of a major sculpture some five metres high. It was to be installed at the end of the main walk, extending down a gentle slope from the house to the boundary of the property, with a spectacular view of the distant sea beyond. A wooden model of the sculpture had been positioned and viewed from every angle so that the massive piece could be crane-lifted directly on arrival into its appointed place.

'Granite Catamarans on a Granite Wave', 1994, by Stephen Cox, black and white granite, 8 metres long. The stone comes from Kanchipuram in India where the sculptor has set up a studio with a team of assistants. The inspiration derives from local fishermen's boats.

Left 'Temple', 1997, by Allen Jones, steel and mosaic, 8 metres high. The colour range of the tesserae is intended to suggest movement in the figure on the plinth.

Above 'Fish on a Bicycle' by
Steven Gregory, bronze, 1.77
metres high, one of an edition
of nine. *Right* A five-metre
bench in laminated plywood
by Thomas Heatherwick.

'Bag Men', 1994, by Steven Gregory is a fantasy of alien figures moving aimlessly about the wooded landscape at Hat Hill Copse.

Jeannette Cass, who is responsible for the planting between the house and the woods, takes expert advice to ensure that its development over the years will create harmonious glades and vistas. She is fond of variegated shrubs, and so there is plenty of euonymus ground cover, with clumps of eleagnus planted in informal groups. In March, blue chionodoxa wind their way among the trees, creating pools of light. In April, a dense carpet of daffodils appears and the sculptures seem to float on a bright yellow sea. The same effect recurs in May, only this time it is an ocean of azure bluebells. Many other species of wild flowers have appeared as the damaged trees and vines are cleared, allowing light to reach the woodland floor. One of the truly magical things about these woods is the way in which the sunlight filters down through the trees and is reflected off the sculptures in a constantly changing spectrum of shades, from the cool light of the early day to the gold of evening.

Hat Hill Copse has become a Mecca for museum curators, art critics and collectors from all over the world. On certain days the sculpture garden is open to the general public, who can wander through the trees and come to terms – if they can – with the challenges of modernism. 'We have set up a foundation to manage what we have created here,' says Wilfred Cass. 'Thus, there will be continuity and we like to think, as far as one can see ahead, that this place will continue to encourage the flowering of British sculpture which has been such an exciting feature of the last quarter of the twentieth century.'

SALLY MATTHEWS was born into a family whose life revolved around animals. Her father was a veterinary surgeon, her mother a farmer's daughter, and the family kept and bred animals at home. Being with them made Sally want to draw animals, a talent which later developed into the sculptures she makes today.

It all started, she says, when she visited Grizedale Forest as a student soon after she left college. 'I was given one month's residency in 1987 to make a wild boar, and was soon given more time to increase the herd. I had longed to free my animals from the flat workshop and gallery floors, but Grizedale also made sense of the way I worked and used materials. Working in the forest gave my sculpture the naturalness of animals with us, rather than animals as art.' Perhaps it is because wild boars have long been extinct in England that they play a very lively role in Sally's sculpture repertoire.

'Everyone has their own reasons for using animals in their art, but I always go back to the animals themselves for inspiration. My love of them, their different form, movement, smell and nature, are the reasons for my making them. Their nature, even of domesticated or trained animals, is unpredictable and wild, their presence is always enlivening. I want my work to remind people of our need for animals and the example their nature provides us with. Making the animals, working their structure and realizing them in their surroundings, always brings me back down to earth, and the sculpture takes on its own spirit. When I make sculptures outside, the work is not passive, the place and materials have their own force. I leave a lot of my making to chance – the finding of a piece of wood, the movement

LIVE
ANIMALS
◆
ENGLAND
SALLY MATTHEWS

'Boars in Grizedale Forest'. The creatures, long extinct in Britain, are imagined grazing in what was their natural habitat. As a student, Sally worked at Grizedale Forest.

Above 'Deerhounds'.
Constructed of mud and
graphite on a steel frame.

Left 'Two Cow-Muck Cows' demonstrate a typical transformation
of locally found materials into art. Brought
up on a farm, Sally observed animals at first hand.

Above This sad, bedraggled
horse, set in a forest,
illustrates Matthews' love of
animals. She wants her work
to endear people to animals,
and this one strikingly meets
this aim.

of the cement mixture, the fingerprints, the different materials, the chicken wire showing through.'

Her sculptures are made from a wide variety of materials, ranging from hay, peat and thistledown to scrap metal, concrete and cow dung, mixed with a stabilizing glue. The materials she works with and the process of making have always been important to her. 'Living on a farm, you learn to turn your hand to anything, making things out of what's around, mending and making do. There are always plenty of odd materials lying around to work with. I know my work is not always anatomically correct, but the movement of an animal is unpredictable. I enjoy making them and I feel it is more important to allow myself some mistakes than to burden myself with details.'

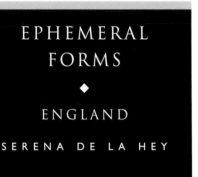

EPHEMERAL FORMS

◆

ENGLAND

SERENA DE LA HEY

SINCE 1992, SERENA DE LA HEY has been rushing from London to the Nevada desert, USA, to Ontario, Canada, to Montevideo, Uruguay, to Normandy, France and to Somerset and Cornwall in England, creating strange, life-size sculptures woven out of willow. She was born in Kenya in 1967; she looks as frail as her sculptures, but has hands that are accustomed to welding.

Before choosing willow as her medium, Serena worked with a blacksmith, making metal sculptures. There were a variety of reasons and influences which persuaded her to change her materials. 'I came back to my home in Somerset, where thatching is an ancient art and trade, and found that everybody was either weaving or thatching. I felt that willow could have even more to offer. In addition, making perky animals and tall swirling figures out of willow needed less strength, much less capital and more innovation. It also enabled me to project my mood into my work: happy, bad tempered, romantic, bossy, angry, active, nostalgic. The shapes reflect inner emotions which are impossible to convey in metal.'

It takes her two or three weeks to complete a sculpture, working with freshly cut willow, each piece being carefully positioned in its chosen surroundings. The site is as important as placing a picture in a frame and when its choice is imposed on her by a client, then the scale of the surroundings becomes the important factor in the design of her work.

Serena de la Hey's figures have an eerie look of skinless bone, vein and muscle. They may look frail, but they project dramatic energy. Whether working with dry or live willow, the reed is laboriously bent and woven, tugged and pulled over a metal frame – which is where Serena's blacksmith training comes into play. When working with live willow, tender green leaves begin to appear in spring, bringing the sculptures to life. Her clients are always concerned about how long the sculptures will last. Serena explains that people are obsessed with longevity, even though life is by its very nature ephemeral. The notion of time is subjective and we tend to use our own lives as a yardstick. The willow sculptures can last up to ten years, even longer if treated with linseed or appropriate wood preservative.

This idea of art and time, of making art as ephemeral as its surroundings, was highlighted by Serena de la Hey in a performance event in the USA. Three figures were constructed in the Nevada desert in collaboration with members of the public. Each year the sculptures were burnt and created anew, becoming an art of resurrection.

Opposite American designer Patrick Dougherty's swirling bamboo construction snakes along the ground, rising in tall arches. A design for fun.

A mysterious figure, fashioned out of willow by Serena de la Hey, lurks in the undergrowth deep in the Lost Gardens of Heligan in Cornwall.

138

EXORCIZING NATURE

◆

IL GIARDINO
SEGGIANO, ITALY

DANIEL SPOERRI

'Warriors of the Night', a fantastic assembly of objects of all sorts, hardly identifiable once fused together with bronze, stand in the pond like a curious flock of flamingos.

THE ROUTE DANIEL SPOERRI'S LIFE TOOK before he reached Tuscany was one full of contradictions, absurdities and fears. Daniel Isaak Feinstein was born a stateless person in the Romanian town Galati. His father was a Romanian Jew who converted to Protestantism, a decision which did not prevent the Germans from murdering him. The young Feinstein was then brought up in Switzerland by his mother and a new father, Spoerri, rector of Zurich University, whose name he takes. Daniel's Italian name was in some ways a passport which would eventually grant him access to an abandoned farm in Tuscany where olive trees, vines, pines, fig trees and laurels had managed to survive in spite of years of neglect. Today it has become his own version of a sculpture garden, simply named Il Giardino.

'If anyone had prophesied that I would one day turn my attention to a garden,' says Daniel, 'they would have proved that they knew little about me; it was unthinkable. Gardens meant to me the obligation to sacrifice my leisure time in clipping the grass, sweating in the heat, pestered by mosquitoes, blisters on my hands, and my mind full of imprecations directed at my aunt. "Nature" was the grass at the edges of paths and I hated it. And still today I couldn't say that I love it. I truly suspect that all human beings are afraid of nature, and that this is why they try so hard to tame, prune and uproot it. It is quite

untrue that primitive peoples loved nature, otherwise they wouldn't have turned their energy, intelligence and imagination toward exorcizing and appeasing the forces of nature with dances, masks and rituals. Culture is a process, as has often been said, of distancing from nature.'

Spoerri chose to distance nature through the placing of objects, the sculptures at Il Giardino. He has long been interested in alternative ways of 'seeing' objects, glueing them to the wall of his minute room in the Rue Mauffetard in Paris: a cup, a bottle, an onion, slices of bread, everyday objects which took on new life as pictures. In his garden, the approach is no different: objects out of context are given a new meaning, yet they are integrated into their natural surroundings. Spoerri declares: 'I am indebted to myself for having held fast to my life's most strenuous effort. I can admit to any and all that it takes the stubbornness of a tractor to be able to realize a thing like this.'

'The Graces – The Seven Ladies of Graz'. Objects replace the heads and incite free associations. Thanks to these uniform busts covered with fissures – suggestive of wounds – Spoerri was called the most surrealistic Neo-realist.

CHAPTER EIGHT

THE TOWN GARDEN

SPACE IN WHICH TO DESIGN a garden is increasingly at a premium, just at the time when more and more people are becoming addicted to the art. Town house garden areas are often extremely small, some positioned at ground level, some exploiting roof terraces. Such gardens are also now used as outdoor rooms for living, and allow scope for exotic planting and garden decoration even within a very small area.

Town garden design involves miniaturizing the available scenery and adapting the plants, both horticulturally and aesthetically. Town councils and architects are not making life easy for the garden lover, but gardeners never give up. If there is no alternative, they will turn to pots, urns and troughs; they will even resort to the artificiality of stone, plastic, cement and paint; and if the worst comes to the worst, they will depend upon a simulated garden of raked sandy areas.

The interesting feature of Hugh and Mary Dargan's American town gardens is the preponderance of raised-bed planting, easy to maintain and offering a better view from within the house.

An overview of the terrace of Leo A. Daly's garden in Washington DC shows its central, seventeenth-century Italian fountain and summer bedding plants in containers.

SECRET
SECLUSION
◆
GENT,
BELGIUM

DENIS DUJARDIN

HOW CAN YOU MAKE a small town garden appear as though it is neither small nor in town? This is quite a challenge, and one which calls for a thorough knowledge of plants before a design is even attempted. Joseph Kosuth is a New York artist, a contemporary of Andy Warhol. About seven years ago, he decided to buy a house for his family in the middle of ancient Gent, one of Flanders' major towns. After restoring the house, he asked Denis Dujardin to tackle the three-hundred-square-metre walled, town garden, which was then a wilderness of maples and elder. It had become a sort of urban jungle, with a fascinating verticality, trees which you could hardly squeeze between packed together side by side.

Denis Dujardin is a Belgian designer who introduces ideas of illusion and deception into his garden plans. He aims to hide boundaries and avoid vistas in order to induce a sense of discovery and a feeling of protective seclusion to his gardens. The challenge in designing a garden in town is to make you forget that the town is there at all, and it is one that Denis Dujardin has risen to in Joseph Kosuth's walled area. The problem he faced was about how much variety and versatility could be achieved in a minimal space. All garden owners are bulimic garden feature lovers – they want shrubberies, lawns, ponds, flowering borders – and those who live in towns and cities are no exception.

Denis explains his design technique here as one of bold, original planting, capitalizing on the garden's existing sense of vertical overcrowding. As he demands maximum performance from his plants, the soil has to be well fed and watered. There is no point planting hungry, thirsty, mature plants and then putting them on a diet. The ultimate aim is to have an undergrowth and overgrowth as lush as possible to help filter the invading noise of the town. Thus, a sinuous path twists and turns between clumps of bamboo and *Hydrangea macrophylla* 'Lanarth White', creating the illusion of a mysterious jungle.

Joseph Kosuth has sober tastes and does not favour a riot of colour, so the plantings are almost exclusively of white flowers, punctuated with some black (Joseph's favourite colour), and the acid yellow of *Alchemilla mollis*. Dujardin even manages to include a small water element – an L-shaped pond – and a neat, practical lawn for sitting out. But he doesn't show off these features: rather, they are cleverly integrated into the general composition, becoming a part of the secrecy and seclusion of the whole.

To obtain an effect of density, colour is not essential, but green is. Bamboo has been used to give height and is combined with generous plantings of *Hydrangea paniculata*. In a sunny clearing, a small water-lily pond breaks up the formality of the taxus hedging.

A general view of the patio shows its displays of lavender, box, catmint and evergreen, low-growing conifers that hold out for as long as they can during the tough Washington winters.

THE CLIMATE IN Washington DC is such that hostesses who entertain guests in their city gardens vie with each other to come up with the most ingenious planting solutions to the problems it poses. Harsh, freezing winters and baking hot summers drastically reduce the available choice of plants for the garden. The average display is usually limited to a few hardy, evergreen shrubs, ball-pruned, and a short period of brilliant flowering spring or summer bedding plants.

Leo A. Daly, a prominent international architect, and his wife, Grega, asked me to help them to plan a new garden. In Washington, gardens tend to be cheek by jowl, so the first problem we had to tackle was just such an over-neighbourly position. The Daly residence is situated just behind that of the British ambassador and beside the garden belonging to Paul Mellon. 'The British and the Mellons have such beautiful gardens,' said Leo, doubtfully.

145

'Don't worry,' I reassured him, 'we won't compete, we'll be different and more architectural in our design.'

No visible boundary separates the Dalys' land from that of the gardens next door. The building of walls is prohibited in this area and hedging is regarded as *passé*, so we resorted to a spectacular seventeenth-century arch of twelve-foot-high stone columns, dressed with purple wisteria and roses, flanked by two weeping cherry trees and under-planted with sword and autumn ferns. From the house, this half circle looks like a stage set, but one alive with plants. There are two other trees on the site, a superb willow oak and a tulip magnolia, whose wide spreading branches protect the garden a little from the full impact of the climate of frosts, extremely hot and humid summers and violent storms.

Above An inviting entry to the sculpture garden is made through a stone doorway; a break in the wall adds depth and interest to the garden and creates two different atmospheres.

Previous pages A bronze sculpture of a seated man by Dame Elisabeth Frink is set amongst baskets of flowers that can be moved around the terrace and planted up to bloom season by season.

Right Dominating the garden, a larger-than-life-size bronze figure of a man by Dame Elisabeth Frink is positioned on a rustic pedestal.

Grega Daly had the original idea of containing seasonal plants for the terrace in large, rustic, hand-woven baskets, in which they were well protected from the weather. The terrace becomes a picture in spring when the baskets are full of azaleas and tulips. As soon as the spring display is over, the baskets are increased in number for summer bedding out. The autumn show is usually created by dahlias or chrysanthemums.

To enable guests to keep their feet dry on their way to the terrace, eighteenth-century stone slabs have been used and planting areas are sunk down between them. The double level of the terrace allows you to look down from the upper terrace to the planted area three steps below. On the top terrace, Grega Daly has arranged her seasonal flowering baskets, whilst on the lower terrace, neat box topiary surrounds low shrubs and standard roses. The peripheral borders are narrow but generously scattered with seasonal bulbs, which give sufficient variety and colour all year round.

The atmosphere of an outdoor living-room is created by a large, fifteenth-century French fireplace at one end of the rectangular terrace and by a glass and stone dining-room filled with exotic plants on the opposite side. In an adjacent, closed-in area, or outdoor room, bronze sculptures of male figures by Dame Elisabeth Frink live a life of their own. These larger-than-life bronzes occupy their own personal garden. Clipped hedges are planted down into the stone floor of this seductive, intimate, mini-sculpture garden, following designs by Leo A. Daly. The general effect of this new-style garden is that of the continuation of indoor life out of doors. Maintenance is a one day a week job, yet the overall appearance of the garden is one of elegance in an entirely original setting.

This overview of the garden shows the island beds of the patio planted with various topiary shapes. The dark tones of the evergreens are in striking contrast to the pale stone used for the hard surfacing.

A WALLED GARDEN

◆

BATH, SOMERSET, ENGLAND

THE REVEREND JOHN ANDREW

In this very protected town garden, the planting is almost exclusively in containers, enabling change and diversity and easy maintenance. Pots of annuals, introduced for spring and summer colour, are easily removed when their show is over.

Opposite Nothing contrived breaks the harmony of this upper level of the garden, accessible via a flight of stone steps. A venerable mulberry tree screens off views from the windows of other houses.

BATH, THE FAMOUS SPA TOWN in south-west England, possesses many beautiful, secret places. This wealth includes a lovely, eighteenth-century house where Queen Charlotte stayed when she visited Bath in 1817, which is now inhabited by the Reverend John Andrew.

Hiding in between six-metre-tall walls is a very elegant town garden, complete with a pond of water lilies and fish. Pots of pelargoniums, fuschias and white impatiens bring light and gaiety to this enclosed scene. Steps lead to a higher level, where a mulberry tree offers its shade and drops its berries on an old paved courtyard. This is a beautiful, traditional town garden design, quite in keeping with the lovely old house which it surrounds.

MASTERS OF URBAN DESIGN

◆

ATLANTA, GEORGIA, USA

MARY &
HUGH DARGANO

Below left On a quatrefoil lawn in Atlanta, blue and white chequered Portuguese pots anchor the corners. The bright blue glass balls on the lawn can be moved around, introducing an element of entertainment.

Below right The centrepiece of a blue-stone patio is ringed by low-growing rosemary, thyme and verbena. Under the stairs, a huge, red-flowering musa forms a shading canopy for a sitting area.

MARY AND HUGH PALMER DARGAN are two young designers working in Atlanta, Georgia, an area of the USA where walled town gardens with lush planting are fashionable and in demand. In order to make the gardens easy to maintain and attractive all the year round, the Dargans' designs are characterized by raised beds in which good drainage helps plants to perform well. They also favour large-leaved, textural plants such as the evergreens flowering banana (*Musa*) and hedychium, which are given colour by interplanting with, for example, spectacular crinum bulbs. One of the Dargans' trademarks is a paving mix of bluestone and brick, which they coordinate with the walling of the raised beds, giving integrity to the overall design. The town gardens represent a perfect combination of attractiveness and practicailty for their discerning but busy owners.

A bull-nosed, brick-edged swimming pool features a black plaster interior, making it look more like a lagoon or a garden pond. *Ophiopogon japonicus* (mondo grass) echoes the dark green and fine texture of the eyead palm (sago) clumps that accentuate the pond.

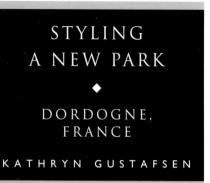

STYLING
A NEW PARK

◆

DORDOGNE,
FRANCE

KATHRYN GUSTAFSEN

KATHRYN GUSTAFSEN does not design for design's sake, but aims to penetrate and evoke the philosophy of the firm or product of the client for whom she is working.

She designs mostly for corporations and for city projects, of which the L'Oreal company is one interesting example. Located in the suburbs of Paris, the factory expresses the preoccupations of the L'Oreal cosmetics firm – precision, science and beauty. Kathryn has translated these ideals into a garden displaying a model of the earth in the form of a female body. I have included her work here among private gardens because her innovative style, which has won her more than fifty commissions in the United States, France and England, will certainly have an impact on private garden designers.

Gustafsen started her career as a fashion stylist, working in Paris and New York, and enjoyed a few years of success and fun designing clothes for wealthy clients. But in 1980 she decided to call it a day and she registered on the landscape architecture course at Versailles. Her first commissions were in France, then she expanded into Great Britain, where she was winner of the Jane Drew Prize (the UK's second largest cash prize for architecture), creating a stir in the profession. New commissions warranted a third office in Seattle. Kathryn now runs her consultancy and design business from three offices, where qualified architects and designers translate her clay models into plans. I think she is probably the only garden designer who visualizes and produces her designs in three-dimensional clay representations – more evocative for the client, she says, than flat-plans and sketches. American-born Kathryn is so cosmopolitan that when she says she is going home, I have not been able to make out where exactly she is off to.

Today she has international commissions from industry and town planners, including the redevelopment of the two-hundred-and-twenty-acre Crystal Palace site in London, the creation of a botanical garden in Wales and the design of several other recreational sites. She is industrious, she has vision and she is fun to work with, say her collaborators, all characteristics which definitely show up in Kathryn Gustafsen's work.

Right A brick waterfall crosses the canal at right angles and ends in an angular pool. Evergreens are planted in a formal arrangement on the terraced land either side of the waterfall.

Above Water is the essential element of Gustafsen's park landscape at Terrasson in France. Water jets shoot up from the brick surfaces edging a long canal that appears to continue through to the landscape beyond.

THE GARDEN PARK

◆

MUNICH, GERMANY

ROSEMARY WEISSE

In Westpark, Weisse has laid 'garden paths' as opposed to walkways, an entirely new approach to a public park. The path is edged with plantings of *Verbena bonariensis*, *Coreopsis verticillata* and golden-rod (*Solidago*).

THE DESIGN OF PUBLIC PARKS has radically changed in recent years. The old, formal layouts have disappeared, replaced by designs which emulate those of domestic gardens and provide plantings which are both instructive and enjoyable.

Many of our old city parks are now overshadowed by towering buildings, encroached upon by roads, edged with cemented pavements. It takes more than forty years for most trees to mature, yet in the city the average lifespan of a street tree may be only ten years. Today, many of the great nineteenth-century parks, such as Central Park in Manhattan, are in decline. Trees set apart on mown lawns cannot regenerate themselves, but they are not being replaced by planted saplings. Many of the parks once conceived as lungs for a city are disappearing beneath parking lots, skating rinks, swimming pools and museums.

The garden designer Rosemary Weisse not only understands these problems, but envisages a way to avoid them in her informal planting scheme for an area of Westpark in

155

Stretches of meadow grass with patches of self-sown annuals – Oriental poppy (*Papaver orientale*), ox-eye daisy (*Leucanthemum vulgare*), white and lilac-pink dame's violet (*Hesperis matronalis*) and *Polemonium caeruleum* – make this town park look like a stretch of peaceful countryside.

Munich. In her design, she has not attempted a formal, organized plan. There is no grouping of plants in borders, in fact it almost seems as though the designer has forgotten, or chosen to ignore, all the traditional rules of plant and colour associations. The result is mass planting in casual communities: *Miscanthus sinensis* socializes with *Stipa gigantea*, rising out of the ground in huge clumps. Clusters of spreading spring plants mingle together, such as the strongly fragrant *Dianthus gratianoplitanus* among the snow-white *Iberis sempervirens* and the blood-red *Tulipa tarda*. All will probably be smothered in summer by encroaching *Alchemilla mollis*, but nobody minds because it simply precludes the problem of weeds. Snails and elder are not partial to this habitat, either.

Rosemary is familiar with the colourful wild flora of central Europe, such as the sturdy flowering ground-cover plants of the rocky alpine slopes, and she uses them to great effect in her scheme at Westpark. She understands the plants she uses and is familiar with their

likes and dislikes. Her planting doesn't follow a traditional layout of tall at the back, short at the front, but is as random as it would be in the wild, so that scattered clumps reappear here and there without special attention being paid to their neighbours' colour. For anyone with a keen eye and interest in the natural habitats of plants, Westpark is an ecological lesson.

Stones and rocks have been cleverly handled in the park design. They are not piled up to resemble a mountain avalanche, but laid in gradual slopes where ground-cover plants tolerant of dry, infertile soil, such as irises and *Asphodeline lutea*, are happy without irrigation. Paths are not stark and wide, they just beckon you on through drifts of hemerocallis, valerian or nepeta, past an odd poppy or iris that has just popped up where its seed falls. The resulting garden looks very natural, a sort of 'plant sociological system', as Rosemary Weisse describes it.

Rocky outcrops of *Campanula poscharskyana* and bearded iris in the foreground are part of a natural-looking landscape in the park.

CHAPTER NINE

THE PATIO GARDEN

PATIO? SUNDECK? YARD? The choice and the name just depend on whereabouts you live in the world. Patios are not only attractive additions to the home, but also the answer to many domestic problems, such as a shortage of living space. A patio is inexpensive, elegant and adds an extra, outdoor room to the house. And it is not only the town-house dweller who is keen on a stone-floored garden: even in country homes, designers are linking houses to gardens with patios, providing new scope for 'exterior decorators'.

National habits differ, climates differ and styles differ, so each country has a different approach to patio design. Countries with well-shaded patios are traditionally those where sheltering from the heat is the main objective, but more recently, even northern countries are developing a taste for exterior living spaces. It is interesting to note that a few years ago you would never have seen pavement cafés in England as you do on the continent; the British kept their indoor life hidden, but now they too are eating and drinking in the open, 'patioing'.

The uses of patios are diverse. 'A nice way to have your friends in for a barbecue or a cocktail,' says an American lady. 'A safe place for the children to play in the fresh air,' says a Swiss mother. 'A good place to sit and rest,' says a Spanish gentleman. 'An ideal place in which to garden,' says an English lady. From my French perspective, the bonus of a patio is that it provides an attractive feature to look at, even from indoors.

Left The granite floor of a patio designed by Jose de Yturbe contrasts with dark woodland. The pillars painted with faded Mexican pink emphasize the informality. *Right* A croquet lawn of Astroturf laid out on a flat roof in a New Mexico garden designed by Martha Schwartz.

STRIDENT, DARING COLOUR is the hallmark of Jose de Yturbe's work in Mexico, and it is in designs for patio gardens that he really indulges this taste. His colourful 'outdoor/indoor' rooms are invigorating designs which imply communication and entertainment. Although his use of colour is extremely vivid, it is never vulgar, and his vibrant, smooth-walled, roofless enclosures make a complete break from more traditional patio design.

His work is part of a contemporary Mexican trend which has been dubbed 'emotional architecture'. This regional and vernacular style is derived from popular building elements such as porticos, patios, fountains and plazas, features taken from Spanish colonial, Moorish and pre-Colombian architecture. Elements derived from nature are also used, drawn from the landscape in which the buildings are situated – volcanic stone, clay, wood and palapas.

The colours used in this architecture are also taken from the broader environment, in particular from the clothing worn by the local people. Luis Barragan was the first modern architect to introduce the colours of the Mexican marketplace into his work. He translated the bright pinks, yellows and purples of toys, fruit, candies, candles and clothes onto vast expanses of painted wall. Describing his approach, Barragan called colour 'a complement

Left In an enclosed patio, stark simplicity and geometric design are Jose de Yturbe's trademarks.

Right Another of Yturbe's dramatic floorings features pebble mosaic surrounding bold concrete circles, arranged within a grid.

Right An incline is terraced and planted with strongly outlined maguey plants – a tribute to sun, sky and Mexican vegetation.

Above A stone-paved patio is dominated by a single tree, and dramatically lit after dark.
Below An orange, yellow and white façade is perfectly reflected in a discreet pool.

A patio planted up in containers opens gently onto a jungle area of a Mexican garden.

to architecture. It can be used to widen or enclose a space. It is also imperative for adding that touch of magic to an area'. This colour lesson is one which the next generation of Mexican architects have taken to heart, and none more so than Jose de Yturbe, who has advanced Barragan's techniques a step further.

Yturbe's houses are characterized by the privacy and serenity of their spaces; he is known for achieving a sense of complete isolation from the world around. In many cases, the use of peripheric walls around the property line is prohibited, so landscaping is all that's available to ensure the privacy of a house, or to protect it from noise or from visual contamination.

The most important idea to understand about Yturbe's landscaping is that the garden is designed to be left to grow freely, to allow the house to mature within its landscape, so that in time the two unite. As they age hand in hand, the landscape and house become one – the only way for a home to grow old with dignity. In some of his designs, made as long as thirty years ago, plants have actually invaded the built architecture and have now become an integral part of the whole.

MARTHA SCHWARTZ'S GARDENS are perhaps better described as 'open air decor', but in their making she nevertheless tackles and resolves garden problems in practical and humourous ways. She is quite definitely a gardener, but one who sometimes chooses to employ no soil, no water, no planting remit and no garden maintenance. Instead, she uses a lot of imagination, making her one of the most talented and controversial of contemporary garden designers.

I went to meet Martha Schwartz in her vast studio just outside Boston, where she works with twelve young, aspiring garden designers. I really wanted to find out why someone who is known as one of the leaders in her field seems to enjoy designing 'virtual' gardens as well as the more conventional, horticultural varieties.

Today, most city buildings have flat roofs, totally windswept, which architects and their clients need to use and enhance. Designs made for these barren surfaces need to take into

TRICKING
THE EYE

◆

BOSTON,
MASSACHUSETTS,
USA

MARTHA SCHWARTZ

In the garden of the Dickenson Residence in Santa Fe, New Mexico, water channels mosaiced with tiny, coloured glass tiles shimmer in the sunlight. The channels, lined with metal to amplify the sound of flowing water, connect to four fountains.

Two more views of the
Dickenson garden show how
different it looks at night,
illuminated from the inside of
the fountains. In a
chequerboard design, apple
trees between the fountains
are anchored with white
marble rocks.

In the Splice Garden at the Whitehead Institute, raked sand surrounds neat topiary balls – which won't need pruning, as they are made of plastic.

account restrictions such as the difficulties of importing earth, of watering and often of non-existent budgets for the subsequent maintenance of the garden. Symbolic, *trompe l'oeil* gardens are the answer to such limitations. Schwartz's materials are cement and plastics – stone is too costly for a project which often has to have budget approval from a board of directors, a manager or a council. Sometimes limited plantings of trees or shrubs in specially constructed containers is possible, but even these have to be answerable to climatic hazards. Colour is an important element of Martha's work: royal blues, sunset reds and oranges to accentuate the designs and white marble rocks to anchor trees.

Her projects are often humourous: her Bagel Garden, designed in 1980, for example, features a dozen mixed bagels coated with polyurethane and sited on purple aquarium gravel. The Bagel Garden is, she says, meant to be ironic, fun, contrasting with the obvious and traditional. Martha's conception, I should say, perception, of a garden is to create a design which relates to the site, the client and the environment. She classifies her work as structural gardening, 'borrowed from nature', and sees no reason to try to justify this conceit.

Another good example of her work is the Splice Garden, an ode to 'better living through chemistry'. The windswept, nine-storey rooftop garden in Cambridge, Massachusetts, is part of an imaginative art collection assembled for the Whitehead Institute, a microbiology research centre. Along with its limited space, the floor of the courtyard was constructed with a concrete decking system that could not hold weight. There was also no source of water for the rooftop, no maintenance staff, and a low budget, precluding the possibility of introducing living plants. However, it was entirely possible to convey a sense of a planted garden by providing enough signals for the site to 'read' as a garden, a feat in which Martha Schwartz excels. She wanted the narrative of the garden to relate to the work carried out by the Institute. The garden became a cautionary tale about the danger inherent in gene splicing: the possibility of creating a monster.

This garden *is* a monster, the joining together like Siamese twins of gardens from different cultures. One side is based on a French Renaissance garden, the other on a Japanese Zen theme. The elements that compose these gardens have been distorted: the rocks typically found in Zen design are composed of topiary pompoms from the French garden. Other plants, such as palms and conifers, are in strange and unfamiliar associations. Some plants project off the vertical surface of the wall, whilst others teeter precariously on

Only artificial materials are used in the Splice Garden, as no earth or water was practicable on the rooftop space.

the wall's top edge. All the plants in the garden are plastic. The clipped edges, which double as seating, are rolled steel covered in Astroturf. The green colours, which are the strongest cues that this is a garden at all, are composed of coloured gravel and paint. Her intent was to create a visual puzzle for the scientists who occupy this building.

Colour has become Martha's mainstay, colour which transforms and enriches her cement constructions, turning them into magical, entertaining garden symbols. Six different projects are on her drawing board at the moment – for the USA, China, Germany and the UK. Even private clients are taking an interest in these non-living gardens for certain areas of their properties, such as pools, patios and entertaining areas, in order to reserve the maintenance of planting schemes for chosen appropriate sites elsewhere in the gardens. To this approach to gardening Martha Schwartz gives her wholehearted approval.

To the question of the life span of these fun gardens, Schwartz answers: 'As long as you enjoy them. It takes less time and money to give them a new coat of paint than it does to weed and prune my garden.' But I still can't help thinking about the birds, the bees and the butterflies who like to inhabit gardens and whose lives are real, not virtual.

A corner of the Splice Garden shows its contrasting areas of design that constitute an entertaining 'virtual' garden in an otherwise bleak space.

CHAPTER TEN

GARDENING IN GRAVEL

DURING MOST OF the twentieth century, gardeners were quite constrained in their choice of plants, having to confine themselves largely to the available safe, climate-hardy varieties. Today, they are more adventurous in their selections, sometimes even taking considerable risks with unusual plants. The visiting of gardens in other countries and the free access to information in the horticultural press have created a demand for a more exotic brand of plants which, to our surprise and pleasure, are turning out to be quite adaptable to most gardens.

The challenge today is not merely in what you plant, but where and how you plant it for the best chance of its survival. With the arrival of more Mediterranean plants, for example, gardeners have adapted their planting to the needs of species which cannot tolerate being waterlogged. Encouraged further in this pursuit by the problems of drought now prevalent in the northern hemisphere, gardeners are experimenting extensively with gravel gardens, dry gardens in which these plants respond and flourish.

Right A view of Beth Chatto's garden in Essex shows how the plants are allowed to encroach on the gravel in soft curves.

Left In a corner of John Brookes' garden in Sussex, an *Acer pensylvanicum* sheds its golden leaves while a pensive boy seems to be waiting for the nymphaea to flower.

A JEWEL BOX

◆

COLCHESTER, ESSEX, ENGLAND

BETH CHATTO

'THE GRAVEL GARDEN is not irrigated, it is a horticultural experiment where we hope to learn which plants survive extreme conditions.' This sign greets visitors entering an area of Beth Chatto's garden in Colchester. It had been a car park, but she decided to convert it into a gravel garden in the spring of 1992.

Beth Chatto's garden is situated in one of the driest parts of England, which receives an annual rainfall of only twenty inches. Irrigation bans imposed because of low rainfall have been creating more and more problems and frustration for gardeners in many parts of the world as the years go by, and the creation of a specific place for special plants with minimal irrigation requirements seemed urgent. The making of the dry gravel area in Beth Chatto's garden was preceded by extensive preparation and with the benefit of much gardening experience. For example, back in 1975, Beth had plucked up her courage and set off with a van loaded with unusual plants to one of the Royal Horticultural Shows. The plants were mainly drought resistant and many were those which retained their silver foliage in winter. The success of her plants was instantaneous. Her exhibits were awarded ten consecutive gold medals at the Chelsea Flower Show and in 1988 she received the Victorian Medal of Honour for outstanding services to horticulture and an honorary doctorate at the University of Essex.

In spite of being well prepared for undertaking the gravel garden, Beth had qualms about how her plants would react to their new environment and whether it was too

Left The wide gravel walk –
not a path – sweeps around
the deeply planted borders of
what was once the parking lot
of Beth Chatto's garden. The
planting is dense and varied,
with height and colour
controlled.

Right Here and there a single
plant is allowed to seed itself
and make a statement.
Verbascum is an ideal
example, tall but never
staked, standing erect against
a dark green background.

Purple alliums and tall wands of eremurus in a sprinkling of pink papavers are ideal plants to enjoy their gravel bed, which keeps them free from frost and water-logging during the winter. This planting is not labour intensive as the bulbs are left to naturalize and the papaver re-seed spontaneously.

ambitious to try to establish Mediterranean species in a variable English climate, where severe drought can alternate over the months with bitter winds or drenching downpours. The whole project started with the propagation of the necessary plants, and with the meticulous preparation of the soil on the site. Then came the elaboration of the picture she wanted to convey. It promised to be an exciting adventure, although at first it seemed a vast undertaking. The empty car-park space had only one redeeming feature: a long, twelve-foot-tall Leyland cypress hedge protecting the area from biting north-east winds. A narrow, existing border of silver plants at its base was an encouraging feature, as the plants looked happy in spite of the dry, hungry soil.

The soil was broken up and decompacted two feet deep with a tractor. This deep penetration of the soil was to prove most beneficial for the establishment of the plants. On smaller areas, Beth was content with double diggings. The land was lightly forked over

and rolled. Then areas to be designed as planting islands were marked out using hosepipes. This method was used, firstly, because the general overall effect becomes clear with a hosepipe contour, which is easy to adjust and, secondly, because it's so much fun doing it this way. Leaving the hosepipes in place, these planting areas were then fed with bonfire waste, well rotted manure and compost. These nutrients were not wasted on the walking areas which weave through the garden, where the earth was simply re-compacted. A big tank of water was conveniently placed in the centre of the garden so that every plant could get a real soaking before retiring to its dry life.

The placing of the plants was the most exciting part. Beth did not aim at colour harmony, but more specifically at contrasts of height and of flowering periods. Memories of dried-up river beds influenced her as she made gently sinuous walks around the planted island beds. The overall effect was to make the islands look informal, even if now and again

Eryngium giganteum and *Acanthus spinosus*, two prickly customers that complement each other – acanthus, with its rigid, plum-coloured rods and eryngium, with its wide-spreading branches.

Symphony in violet with *Allium christophii* and *Lavandula stoechas pedunculata*, often referred to as 'French lavender', probably because it is indigenous in Provence, where the flowers are more often pink.

they did encroach onto the walking area. Once she was satisfied with the planting, gravel was generously laid down to cover beds and walking areas alike. It is a nice feeling walking on fine pea-gravel, especially in winter when the rest of the garden is really mushy.

It has become apparent that plants in gravel retain their flowers over a longer season than those in traditional settings. Freak blooms appear in the gravel, such as a spray or two of *Lychnis coronaria* in flower in October and flowering bergenia going strong for months. In November, plants like artemisia, perovskia and achillea die down and the exposed gravel is much more attractive than bare soil, also acting as a protective mulch during winter. Many of the plants retain good foliage all the year round, and attractive seed heads are not cut down. Graceful grasses are a foil to flowering bulbs, beginning in winter with *Crocus Tommasinianus,* scilla, chionodoxa and snow-white galanthus. Freshly cut-back herbaceous plants poke their heads through mats of thyme, adding to the beauty of the overall picture.

Beth Chatto admits that her planting may appear chaotic to the observer of correct rules of harmony, but in what she calls her planted 'jewel box', she has created a living tapestry woven into a tissue of greys, greens and bronzes. From this basic colour palette emerge the bold effects of her star performers: giant chives with ball-like heads of pink or blue; tissue-paper-like pink poppies; the illuminating candelabra of *Verbascum Olympicum;* or the all-year-round favourite, *Euphorbia characias wulfenii.* Elsewhere, clusters of the very foreign-looking *Lavandula stoechas,* with its mauveish-pink heads, are well shown off by their neighbour, the silvery santolina.

The beauty of this type of garden is that it can be made on virtually any site of any size. Although the planting in Beth Chatto's garden is very Mediterranean, hardly any plants have been lost due to cold or frost; even those which may have had their tops bitten off have responded to the warmer spring temperatures and revived. As a result, walking through the gravel garden is like entering quite another country and another clime.

WE NEED TO MOVE ON. Gardeners are always doing the same old thing, based on Edwardian garden principles. We need some new thinking, new ideas and techniques,' says John Brookes. 'We have got into a herbaceous border/striped lawn/topiary rut. We must move on.'

Walking around his garden in high summer, you could easily imagine you were far away on some sun-baked Greek island, or in a *maquis* garden tucked away in the south of France. But we are at Denmans in West Sussex, where Brookes has lived, gardened and created his Design School since 1980.

It was during a holiday on the island of Delos in Greece that the late Joyce Robinson, the previous owner of Denmans and the creator of its garden fifty years ago, discovered that many plants – amongst them the most beautiful – can live and prosper without the overfeeding and overwatering with which we have been conditioned to indulge them. John Brookes joined Joyce in the creation of this new style, new habitat garden, adding his design expertise to her vision. The Mediterranean feel has been interpreted in a gravel gardening technique of informal plantings which get the maximum drainage and maximum protection from frost and damp.

Far from constituting traditional beds, the plants are arranged in new associations that filter into the gravel areas, sometimes divided by grassed pathways. The gravel 'beds' just

An expanse of lawn in front of the house is broken up by an island bed of *Euphorbia characias* that provides structure with its animated green flowers in spring and early summer.

Above Contrasts in colour and form make an interesting impact with catmint in the foreground, *Asphodeline lutea* and *Allium (Nectaroscordum) siculum*, *Fagus sylvatica* 'Purpurea Pendula', *Photinia x Fraseri*, *Euphorbia characias* and ceanothus in the background.

Opposite Self-seeding is at its natural best in an area where poppies create delightful splashes of pink and red in a bed of anthemis.

seem to occur naturally throughout the garden. The effect is what Joyce Robinson used to call one of 'glorious disarray'. Here and there we find a mound of grass, but it is never a lawn, just a restful green place, sometimes incorporating a tree and bulbs surrounded by gravel.

Since taking the garden over from Joyce, John has made changes, not because he didn't like what she did, but just because 'I am me and she was she – as you might say'. Add time – the fourth dimension of a garden – during the passing of which trees get too big, plants die and so on, and of course it all changes. Gardening is not static and John Brookes has no qualms about removing a tree which has outgrown its space if it is interfering with the overall design.

One aspect of garden design which Brookes enjoys is the use of shape and pattern. This is achieved by his choice of plants – sedum, perennial grasses (very fashionable now the world over), and various sages. But he also uses annuals, because they have such a spontaneous appearance in the gravel, especially *Eschscholzia californica*. Bulbs also respond well to gravel, naturalizing faster than when planted in soil: chionodoxa, scilla and *Ipheion uniflorum* make lovely coloured patterns at Denmans.

'If I have added anything to the garden, it is rationalization of the outline of the grass and planted area of the gravel massings, so that beneath the seemingly random appearance of the plant groups, there is still a strong design.' John hates wiggly patterns, preferring a line which flows. This type of garden is, of course, at the other end of the spectrum to a formal layout. Not that he has anything against a more traditional approach, he just feels he does what is appropriate now, as opposed to what was appropriate before.

'Increasingly,' he says, 'I am pulling away from the metaphor of "Mediterranean" when applied to this type of garden. It just so happens that many of the plants from that region like our well-drained soil and comparatively mild climate. But then so do many of our own native plants – the caper spurge (*Euphorbia lathyris*), butchers broom (*Ruscus aculeatus*), Tutsan (*Hypericum androsaemum*), the guelder rose (*Viburnum opulus*), the wayfaring tree (*Viburnum lantana*), the spindle tree (*Euonymus europaeus*) and the field maple (*Acer campestre*). But I am also looking at how plants associate in nature and I am trying to copy this.

'I have found that by introducing another medium – that of gravel – I can get away from the lawn and border effect. By planting in this semi-wild way amongst the gravel, allowing air between the plant masses, I can create a far looser effect, which is not so studied. Planting in gravel is an easy job: one simply scrapes it away to dig a hole. As for weeding – a real pleasure and precious little of it.

Above A refreshing expanse of two-height mowing creates an area of flowering meadow.

Opposite Clematis montana invades the brick archway, creating a frame of intense colour at the entrance to the garden.

181

Above Mature trees protect the garden from the wind and surround a clearing with a small, well-defined pond. *Below* Tree lupins and euphorbia spill over onto the gravel.

'I have also eliminated a certain amount of cultivation, and by using plants which like my type of soil, I don't need to feed them either. What I do is condition the soil to hold more moisture in summer, since we dry out very quickly. I dig in plenty of organic matter when planting within the gravel area to eliminate watering. I hope my form of Joyce's "glorious disarray" will seem a more Sussex arrangement. I don't want my garden to look like somewhere else – I want it to be of its place.'

John's garden has shed its insular look and rather conjures up new scenery, new styles, achieved by clever planting. Even when he has introduced quite un-English elements, such as a river bed of graded pebbles to give an effect of flowing water (a several-hundred-year-old Japanese technique but now very modern), it still looks beautifully in place with a very English thistle, stately verbascum, iris (of which he is most fond), colourful foxgloves and proud red-hot pokers (*Kniphofia*).

John is very keen on the garden in winter, perhaps because then he doesn't have visitors, but more still as it is a time when the evergreen bones of the garden really show up, dotted with the first flowering treasures of wintersweet, *Iris unguicularis* and hellebores, which bloom so profusely. John Brookes is certainly one of the most consistently innovative of the English gardeners, and Denmans continues to change and to develop as the years go by.

K ATIA DEMETRIADI'S GRAVEL GARDEN near Guildford is for walking about in at will: it has no paths or defined planting beds. It is quite different from the more formal, partitioned gardens we became more accustomed to in the twentieth century. Katia's garden is also a space with a Mediterranean character which reminds her of her native Greece. Even in winter, it manages to give the feeling of a warmer climate.

The site of the garden presented problems, as it slopes quite a lot on two sides and underneath there is a large cesspit and numerous pipes. It also dries very quickly, as the soil is sandy and the land faces south, catching the sun all day. The problem of the slope was solved by building a dry-stone wall (from sandstone, which is local) on two sides to make the area more or less level. Katia discovered that the shallow top soil did not pose a problem since gravel plants don't have deep roots. A spruce and a eucalyptus were already growing there, so she decided to work around them.

The gravel she used is a special mixture from Dorset which includes some small rocks of Cornish slate and a mixture of large and small pebbles. Terracotta pots of various sizes and two stone benches contribute to the garden's Grecian style. An old bath came in handy as a makeshift pond for water plants. The general planting in the gravel is mostly of sun-loving, evergreeen shrubs and perennials, with an emphasis on winter colour. Little poppies and evergreen *Erigeron mucronatus* pop up anywhere they like in the gravel, along with spring bulbs: crocus, tulips and narcissi, all species which look natural growing there. The plants show up unashamedly in the gravel itself, with no edgings, no crowding and without particular regard for vistas through the garden. In fact, you have to be a true plant lover to create such a garden.

Exotic-looking plants can be really hardy if planted in well-drained soil. Phormium, yucca and *Fatsia japonica* are wonderful plants for this sort of garden, as they keep their shape and colour in winter and don't have to be pruned (which is a blessing for many 'secateur-shy' gardeners). Katia has stayed loyal to Mediterranean varieties for the shrubs and perennials that flower regularly in summer. Cistus, for example, are not demanding – they're never really thirsty and are quite content with poor, gravely soil. Agapanthus is quite resistant if covered in winter, as is the blue haze of perovskia and the prolific artemisia. Grasses are equally well used in the garden, which grows various *Stipa* and bamboos.

For extra colour in the summer, Katia has not been afraid to bed out fiery reds, planting geraniums, zinnias and canna lilies, as is the practice in all southern gardens. The garden is also full of butterflies, says Katia, because chemicals are not on her agenda.

Above and left Grasses, yucca, phormium and iris emerge from between smoothly rounded stones that complement the gravel and act as natural sculptures.

A LANDSCAPE IN MINIATURE

◆

SUNNEYMEDE HAMPSHIRE, ENGLAND

HENRY CLYNE

The zig-zagged streak of the lightning walk makes an interesting pathway across the dry gravel area of the garden. It may be inspired by Japanese or Chinese garden design, or be an invention by Clyne.

HENRY CLYNE'S GARDEN in Hampshire is officially called Sunneymede, although he himself dubs it 'memories from my travels in China, Japan, Iceland and elsewhere'.

The garden is built on a slope and is best viewed from the top of the incline. Designed on Japanese gardening principles, scenes from different countries have become translated into a series of dry landscapes, made from local materials, mostly flintstone. The reminiscences it represents have made it a personal garden. It is also a low-budget garden, created by Clyne during his retirement using gravel, sand, scrap rubble and a few items purchased over the years.

From the raked sand garden, the ground drops in a series of terraces, characteristic of Far Eastern design, into the back garden. The first terrace features a 'streak-of-lightning walk' – a series of wooden zig-zags which provide access to the garden for weeding or planting, and compose a rapid through-route if you walk across the centres only, which are just a step apart. Generally, the terraces are all planted to reinforce the impression of their curved shape. On the extreme left, on the paved terrace, is a viewing platform from which you can see under the flagstone bridge to the pond beyond.

If Henry Clyne had lived in any other part of the country, his garden would have been quite different. It was the flint soil created by the moraine of ancient ice movements which suggested the creation of a glacier-garden. The rough silver and black surfaces of the land lend themselves to the construction of areas following the original flow of the glacier, making a stoney, dry garden.

The garden's dry mountain stream is an area of wild primroses and rough growth, with only the semblance of a stone path, as if it were accidental, worn by circumstances, say in the Malvern Hills. Here you can 'become' the stream by picking your way down carefully from stone to stone. At the foot is a flat stone on which to pause and see the Moss Gardens from below and take in the view of the 'sea' ahead – in fact, of course, a completely dry area.

A 'viewing terrace' of large flint stones is positioned above conifers that mark the descending steps. Each small area is designed in a different colour gravel, creating contrasting effects.

Choisya ternata 'Sundance' and small, golden-leaved *Buxus aurea* lighten up the descent to the box area. A cortaderia adds height to the sloping background.

CHAPTER ELEVEN

WATER, WATER EVERYWHERE

MANY PEOPLE ARE now including water features, some very modest, in their gardens. They may be inspired by the grand water gardens of the past, such as Islamic enclosed courtyards with water running along mosaiced canals, or French classical gardens where large expanses of water reflect the grand, awe-inspiring architecture of the day.

In fact, water engineers from the earliest civilizations through to those of the last century knew much about water flows, volumes, dispalcement and display. Some Victorian texts describing the technicalities of moving water are still relevant today. Much of this basic knowledge has been marginalized as improved technology of pumps and control systems takes on an increasingly important role, but designers now have an unprecedented range of options, both old and new, when creating water features.

The art of designing with water was also greatly influenced by Italian techniques brought to France by generations of craftsmen and used in the building of large-scale water pools, canals and fountains. In the early nineteenth century, the Romantic movement in England introduced more natural-looking water scenes into the landscape, and it is this fashion in particular which is the basis for many of the water features we see today.

Below The water splashes over boulders into a pool in one of Isabelle Greene's magical designs in the USA.

Opposite Still waters bordering the grassed areas of Jacques Wirtz's garden in Belgium reflect the intense shades of green of the foliage planting.

Green reflections in still water mirror the impeccable symmetry of this swimming pool design.

THE DESIGN OF A SWIMMING POOL has always been regarded as completely separate from that of the rest of a garden. Usually rectangular and with hard surface sun-decks, pools are as divorced from nature as bath-tubs. However, Isabelle Greene, one of California's most prominent landscape designers, has spurned such stark, unnatural-looking pools. She has worked instead with the existing garden backdrops of trees and shrubs to create pools which appear to have just happened in natural depressions in the landscape.

In Montecito, the pool she has designed is so beautiful, so cleverly constructed, that even the ducks and woodland animals come down for a drink of chlorinated water. Skirting a woodland glade, the pool is sunk in the middle of a ring of natural boulders, most of which were excavated when the pool was under construction. Artificial rocks were added, some of them partly submerged, creating interesting shapes and shadows, and others edge the pool and form entry steps. The making of these artificial rocks is in itself both an artistic and a technical achievement. Shapes and sizes are determined, then latex impressions of existing rock formations are made. The actual casting of the rocks is in lightweight concrete over a fibreglass form; they are then painted with a waterproof, hard-wearing paint which to the eye or to the touch entirely resembles the real thing. These boulders are cleverly mixed in with natural stones and can be cast *in situ*.

The advantage of using artificial rock is that it is lightweight and can be made to any size, shape or colour to blend in with natural local rock. Placed in interesting positions along the edge of the pool, holes can be scooped out for naturalistic plantings of grasses or waterplants. Shallow accesses to the pool are made out of flat, half-submerged stone or by artificially-made stone steps positioned partly underwater. A sandy sloping beach makes another wading-in entry. The 'sand' is made from aggregate of rock, comfortable for walking on.

Large boulders positioned at the deepest end of the pool make attractive diving-boards and an isolated, well-placed boulder becomes a convenient island to rest on. A reflection of trees and shadows is cast by the pool's black plastic lining, well concealed under the stone edging. Flagstones set around the deck area integrate into the natural garden scenery and are planted with Korean grass and clumps of flowers and shrubs which spill over the water's edge.

This swimming pool, conveniently located near the terrace of the house, looks as though it has occurred entirely naturally in the landscape.

Slabs of stone are laid in amongst ground-cover plants to form an entry point to the pool that blends in with the other rocks.

A pool which appears as though it has happened in the hollow of a rock is in fact surrounded by imported and fabricated boulders.

Although totally natural in appearance, the technology which services the swimming pool is impressive: strong skimmers circulate the water, and fallen leaves from the surrounding woodland are cleared from the surface electronically. The temperature is well controlled by a gas heater, which means the pool can be used all year round. The final touch is a stream, which appears to spurt naturally from a nearby spring to run between the rocks and cascade into the pool. It enhances still further the very authentic look of this man-made – I should say, woman-made – haven of natural beauty.

Isabelle Greene has created another of her famous rockscape natural pools at Santa Ynez, amidst the rolling hills of California. The land is dotted with oak trees and covered with golden grasses in late summer, justifying its nickname 'the golden state'.

In a setting of boulders and waterside vegetation, a comfortable, gradual slope of sandy beach – made of an aggregate of small stones and polymer resin – leads into the water of the pool. Birds and deer wade in for a drink at this beach, where it's easy to reach the water. Lined with dark blue plaster which mirrors the surrounding scenery, the irregularly-shaped, elongated pool measures forty by fifty feet. In addition to the rocks, inlets and curves of the pool, a thirty-foot stretch has been designed for swimming lengths, and flat boulders are positioned to jut out at intervals for diving.

The long pool house, with its tiled roof and flat stone deck, shelters among the trees and is elegantly unpretentious in this natural setting. A few feet from the actual pool is an apparent rock water hole (actually a spa), which appears as if a natural spring has cascaded into a gully down from the pool. Pockets of native grasses and flowers are dotted among the boulders and on the slope leading down to the water – German irises, columbines and the flat white heads of achillea all contribute to a lovely, meadow-like framework of plants.

THE GARDEN AT WOBURN was created in six months for Andrew, Lord Howland, the eldest son of Lord and Lady Tavistock. It was intended to be an almost invisible garden which emphasized, rather than diverted attention from, the view of the very lovely English countryside of grazing meadows and distant fields and trees. The plan was for a low-maintenance, bachelor's weekend garden with a swimming pool, barbecue patio, putting green and water feature. Flowers were no real priority, so a simple blue and yellow belt of herbaceous colour was planted around the stone terrace of the house as a colourful introduction to the water garden, unusually sited on the edge of a grazing field. The water garden was literally carved out of the meadow, but not before Andrew had negotiated with his mother, who was not keen to relinquish a piece of her grazing field! Finally, the excavation, designed by Keir Davidson, was lined with clay and rocks were brought in and built up to create a double cascade.

The crowning glory of this feature is Mrs Moss, a life-size bronze horse statue by Philip Blaker, who looks down on the water garden from a high, mown viewpoint. She really deserves this honour; the real Mrs Moss produced fifteen foals, twelve of whom were race winners, including Jupiter Island, winner of the Japan Cup. This is an amazing accomplishment for a mare who cost just 2100 guineas! The water's edge has been planted with a variety of grasses and the inevitable *Gunnera manicata* emerges from between the rocks. Low-cut grass carpets the water's edge, too, but is allowed to grow taller as it extends out towards the fields, where bulbs and wild flowers have been planted and will eventually naturalize.

MINIMUM CARE
AND WATER

◆

WOBURN
BEDFORDSHIRE,
ENGLAND

ANITA PEREIRE

The small water feature, the focus of this low-maintenance garden, is backed by a bronze statue of Mrs Moss, a favourite mare of the Tavistock family. The Abbey's famous parkland is visible in the background.

ROCKSCAPES

◆

QUAKER HILL, NEW YORK STATE, USA

KEIR DAVIDSON

A TWO-HUNDRED-ACRE ESTATE at Quaker Hill, in the State of New York, is the site of one man's dream. What was once abandoned farmland dotted with outcrops of schist rock has become a huge, Zen-inspired, rock, water and woodland garden for establishing a definitive collection of north-east American native plants.

The originator of this ambitious scheme was looking for someone to undertake the project when he happened to come across a book written by Keir Davidson and called *The Art of Zen Gardens*. Davidson's profession doesn't have a specific name; he designs and builds rock and water scenery and is therefore perhaps best described as a 'rockscape designer'. Keir gained his experience and expertise in Japan, where he worked for several years studying the art and technique of Japanese gardens. The man who had the greatest influence on his work was Muso Soseki, a Japanese monk who built Zen gardens in the fourteenth century. His work survives, particularly at Saiho-gi temple in Tokyo, and represents some of the most instructive and subtle rock work ever created. Apart from understanding the properties of different types of rock – their reaction to climatic changes and how they can be cut – a rockscape designer must also be familiar with how water flows over them.

Over a period of fourteen years, Keir built waterfalls, streams and rock features at Quaker Hill, using the beautiful schist, with its mica specks that sparkle in the sun. The rocks are used to create naturalized groups, falls and pond and stream edges, designed on site like a monumental sculpture. The rocks vary in weight, from those that can be carried by hand to large pieces of fifteen, twenty or thirty tons (the weight of three fully-grown elephants). The waterfalls vary in height from three inches to twenty-five feet. Concrete linings are used for the waterfalls and clay for the streams, giving them a more spontaneous, natural look. Pumps are used to recirculate the water. As each waterfall was completed, vegetation was introduced.

Keir Davidson says that his long project will never end, never be finished, as long as the owners' passion lasts. Mature trees are still being planted, some of them of such dimension that roads have to be built to bring them on site. Passions of this magnitude always last.

Below Keir Davidson spent over ten years in New York creating giant water features. This winter scene shows one of his artificial pools surrounded by an imported rock formation.

Opposite Rocks weighing several tons, chosen at quarries and transported and installed on site in New York State, were carefully selected both for their shape and their colour to create an impressive waterfall.

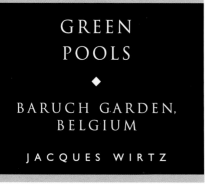

GREEN POOLS

◆

BARUCH GARDEN, BELGIUM

JACQUES WIRTZ

Right These circular, tiered banks give the striking effect of a contemporary topiary. The wide grass walkways and the still moat waters contribute to its sleek, modern appeal.

Above This open garden landscape was once part of the forest. Now a moat establishes the privacy of the property and grassed and hedged embankments create an interesting perspective.

THE BARUCH GARDEN in Belgium is typical of Jacques Wirtz's strong, clear design. Wirtz is an innovative new garden designer, and a master of the art of an all-green garden which avoids cumbersome planting. Wirtz prefers soft, sculptural contours dressed with flowering grasses and trees planted sparsely enough to allow light to shine through the clumps. He manages to create a sense of space by introducing pools of water into his designs, which themselves mirror back the greens of the gardens. In the Baruch garden, Wirtz designs with hedges, creating paths and enclosures, as others design with walls, enabling him to retain the green effect throughout the scheme. Hornbeam, box, yew and, still more original, grasses which create soft, flowing, weedless hedges are the 'bones' of the garden.

Like many of the great gardeners, Wirtz learnt his trade as a youngster in the family garden. This has now become a family tradition, since his two sons, Peter and Martin, have followed in their father's footsteps, running the two companies, Wirtz International (for

the design work), and Wirtz International Architecture (for contracting). Something of an autodidact, Wirtz finds time to embrace many of the arts and crafts, such as music, film, textile design, cooking, botany and architecture. These, together with his frequent trips abroad, have given him a broad, flexible approach to garden design.

Created in the clearing of a wood of pine and beech, the Baruch garden radiates from the house in soft grassed banks, which reduce the landscape's apparent scale and soften its geometrical contours. Wirtz has restricted much of his planting to grasses, which become swathes of ochre in autumn, harmonizing with the warm russet brown of the beeches. Green garden 'rooms' complement the architecture of the house and serve as enclosures for a swimming pool, a flower garden and an oriental-style garden, although the main view from the house is kept open and unhampered. Layed out in sweeping, flowing lines, this is a typical low-maintenance garden, cleverly incorporating a number of unusual water features.

Below Grasses are used in the garden in a most unconventional way, planted in borders that edge a broad, winding grass path.

THE JAPANESE INFLUENCE

T IS NO WONDER that so many garden designers have travelled to Japan to learn from its culture and to bring back new ideas to inspire their own gardens in the West. A Japanese influence is more and more apparent in contemporary gardens, as designers strive to achieve a sense of minimalism, incorporating natural elements such as stone, gravel and water.

The equation is now beginning to become reciprocal as Japanese garden designers become increasingly interested in English plants. As a result, many in Japan are afraid that the classical, traditional Japanese garden will, like the kimono, the futon and the tea ceremony, give way to Western styles.

Young Japanese couples are finding bonsai too expensive and too time consuming to maintain and traditional gardens colourless now that they have been introduced to European consumer goods. They have fallen in love with colourful English gardens, so much so that impatiens are all the rage in Japan and make more impact in small spaces for less money. Japanese lifestyle magazines run photographs and advice about English gardens, and Mistukashi, the big department store in Tokyo, has tripled its sales in the gardening section. Perhaps an admiration for British gardens is a phase which Japan will have to pass through – as other nations have done – before they move on to develop other designs.

Opposite In a Japanese garden design, Marc Keane has planted rolling beds of azaleas. *Left* Richard Haag's design for a small flight of steps allows for tiny ground-cover plants to grow through the lattice of cement blocks.

CROSS CULTURE

◆

ZURICH, SWITZERLAND

STEPHEN SEYMOUR

The eye runs from the lily pond to Lake Zurich and the mountains beyond. The sculpture of a gate in glazed ceramic on a metal frame was made by a Swiss potter.

CREATING GARDENS IN JAPAN enabled Swiss designer Stephen Seymour to appreciate the similarities between Japanese culture and his own. The austerity of Zen is echoed by the simplicity of Calvinism, both relying on a naive feeling for nature and a desire to restrain from excessive decoration. Seymour exploits this common ground in his garden designs in Switzerland, aided by dramatic landscapes similar to those in Japan.

In gardening as in a marriage that crosses cultures, the common values must be highlighted and the differences shaded out in order for the relationship to survive. In Switzerland, the use of natural elements, of which there are plenty, dominates garden design, with stone, gravel, rough wood, water and trees much in evidence. In Japan, these materials are also the basis of all gardens. The Japanese garden is, in fact, composed of many different fixed elements – lanterns, stones, water, fences, walls, fountains, garden houses – each strictly assembled to make a harmonious composition. A Japanese garden is not really natural; only the most beautiful aspects of nature are taken, selected, refined or abstracted.

In their quest for perfection in garden design and construction, the Japanese have developed a highly sophisticated system of pruning to sustain the plant's good health and vigour whilst allowing it to contribute to the harmony of the garden composition. The characteristic spreading shape of a pine tree, with its long, low, lateral branches extended far out from the trunk, is the result of yearly pruning started in its early growth. Each branch extends from the trunk in a series of slight twists and turns, which keep the branch growing in a single course. Whole branches may be cut from the trunk and upper branches thinned out. The purpose of this type of pruning is to allow the sunlight to penetrate down even to the lowest limb of the tree.

A low, spreading shape is considered the most beautiful and most expressive of the pine's personality. The Japanese prefer the branches of any tree to grow in an upward, curving sweep to give the effect of a wing-like feather. The tree should have the appearance of a series of layers of foliage laid irregularly one over the other, with light and air space between each. It is almost as if the foliage were thin, feathery clouds or layers of mist.

Another favoured technique, *karama zukashi*, or 'cloud pruning', creates a tree which appears to be a series of wheels laid one on top of the other. The branches take on the shape of stylized clouds in a Japanese classical painting. This very ancient art is now taking on a new momentum elsewhere in the world and is perhaps set to take the place of classical topiary.

Pine is one of the most popular and widely planted trees in Switzerland, but a very special pruning technique has had to be devised to prevent the heavy snowfall from weighing down the branches and damaging the trees. Stephen Seymour studied in Kyoto with Sano, a master of pruning techniques, over a period of two years, and is now promoting this very ancient technique in modern Switzerland.

A garden which Seymour designed in Zurich was a unique opportunity to create an extensive landscape of ponds, rivers and rock gardens. An unforeseen and dramatic setback in its construction occurred when planning authorities dictated that two storeys of the house had to be removed. This meant that the hill in front of the house obscured the view of the lake in the valley. The only possible remedy was to take a slice off the top of the hill and to create water gardens in the modified landscape. As the house was now sunk lower than its surroundings, a series of rivers flowing towards the house could be created and Seymour was able to construct his water garden on a much larger scale than he had originally envisaged. The result is a garden strongly influenced by Japanese design, yet one which relates perfectly to its scenic Swiss setting.

Surrounding the lily pond, rocks and leaning pine trees create the sort of Japanese scene that Stephen Seymour likes to introduce into his designs.

The distant sea affords what the Japanese call 'borrowed scenery'. The 'cloud' pruned pine between two olive trees on the rocky bank is surrounded by lavender and tropical strelitzia.

O VERLOOKING THE GULF of Porto Vecchio in Corsica, a stretch of land tumbles down to the sea, planted as a perfect example of a garden called *maquis* by the locals, really consisting of overgrown scrubland. Eric Borja was not going to make the mistake of digging out and uprooting the indigenous plants. For once, all the native ingredients of a garden were already there, in the wild olive trees, flashy brooms, evergreen oaks and sprawling junipers growing between lovely, rounded stone boulders. To crown it all, there was a view, but one obliterated by the *maquis* overgrowth.

It was one of those situations where the real talent lay in an ability not to do too much, not to be too clever, not to compete with nature but just to bring it to the fore. Eric's experience in Japan and his study of Japanese gardens was a constant reminder that one can destroy a design by over-zealous remodelling. The neatness found in Japanese gardens is simply obtained by pruning and caring for plants, not by eliminating established species or by over-weeding.

The slope down to the sea needed to be terraced, alternating simple, grassed, sunny areas with stoney viewing-points and a trickling stream cascading into a rocky pond, in Japanese style. A few evergreen oaks had to be sacrificed in order to recapture the view and to accentuate existing areas of natural turf, backed by shrubs. Underwater lighting in the sea itself not only enhances midnight swimming, but also attracts shoals of fish, who seem to enjoy their new, sophisticated nightclub.

An interesting aspect of another of Eric Borja's gardens, this time in the Drone Valley of France, is that it has all the ingredients of a Japanese garden without in any way looking Japanese. The scene is restrained and peaceful, with a gravel raked sea, stone islands and sparse vegetation. To highlight the contrasts in this garden, a pond with a trickling stream

Opposite Silhouetted against the sky, the traditional 'cloud' pruning of this mature pine shows clearly. In the foreground are various neatly pruned shrubs: box, euonymus and lavender are among the many topiaries nestling between the rocks.

Stepping stones provide access across a shallow pool whose banks are planted with azaleas and topiarized conifers.

introduces movement and sound. A tea-garden is spanned by an intricate pebble path, leading to gardens on lower levels. The rocks and boulders encountered on the way down all look as if they just happened to be there, when in fact they were laboriously hauled in from the nearby mountains.

Descending towards the lakes and waterfalls through a succession of horticultural scenes, the eye is constantly straying to hints of Japanese gardens: cloud-patterned tree pruning; a stone puzzle path; a wavy hedge mimicking a Japanese dragon. But Eric Borja's designs are more suggestions of Japanese design than they are actual replicas, proving his ability to adapt the essence of the style to new situations.

Above A stone, carpet-style pathway is made up of cobble stones and small pebbles laid in a criss-cross design.

Right The garden begins under the shade of olive trees near the house. Low, topiarized planting in an outcrop of rocks gives this terrace an informal look. Strelitzia and *Cistus x lusitanicus* emerge from between the rocks.

FOR YEARS, Western gardeners have been importing garden ideas from Japan, learning to cultivate Japanese plants, adopting pruning techniques and the use of rocks and water features and developing a taste for bonsai. In turn, Japanese garden designers are beginning to introduce certain elements of Western gardens into their designs. Marc Keane, a young Canadian living and working in Japan, is one of the designers in the forefront of this trend.

Keane first went to Japan as a tourist guide. He soon became interested in Japanese culture and registered as a research fellow at Kyoto University. Fascinated by Japanese gardens, he realized that to be able to undertake any creative work in Japan he would have to immerse himself in its culture, learning about the arts and Japanese lifestyle – fine art, theatre, graphics, fashion, ink-brush painting and calligraphy; philosophy, food and customs. This was a demanding programme, but before he even dared to place a rock or lay out a path, Marc had to absorb all aspects of Japanese aesthetics. In Japan, design is an art form handed down from generation to generation: learning an art is living an art.

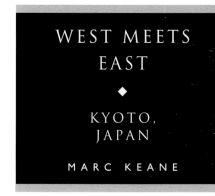

WEST MEETS EAST

◆

KYOTO, JAPAN

MARC KEANE

The rhythmic motion of waves is suggested by this garden designed for contemplation.

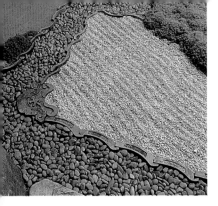

Above This 'drip-line' of rounded pebbles bordered with old roof tiles absorbs rainwater falling from an unguttered thatch roof. Although built for purely functional reasons, it creates a beautiful abstract design in the garden.

Right Although the plants and rammed earth wall are typically Japanese, Marc has laid out this garden in a more European design of island beds.

Opposite A simple, modern wall partitions off a small fountain on a paved terrace. The area is shaded by over-hanging Cape myrtle trees.

His education complete, Marc Keane now designs unique Japanese gardens that incorporate Western elements. One truly European addition to his gardens, for example, is the installation of garden lighting, hardly ever used in Japan except in the form of a carefully positioned stone lantern. West meeting East in his garden designs has produced some very beautiful and entrancing work.

STONE HARMONY

◆

WASHINGTON STATE, USA

RICHARD HAAG

RICHARD HAAG has had many honours bestowed upon him. In 1993, he received the highest award given to a teacher of landscape architecture in the United States, and in 1994 he received the Hubbard Educational Trust Award for Excellence in Landscape Architecture. His achievements are such that he is known in the American north-west as 'the father of landscape architecture'. Yet the most important, philosophical influence on his designs came from a trip to Japan.

Haag was introduced to plants at a very early age and grew up with a deep respect for and interest in the workings of nature. His father was a nurseryman and rasied animals in a rural area. The young Richard roamed the fields and creeks and the wilderness of the landscape around him. By the time he was four years old, he had won a prize for plant grafting, and at six he germinated the seed of his first oak tree. 'My design philosophy now,' he says, 'is that landscape architecture is the ultimate art form, one that treats nature as a lover.'

His observations during his trip to Japan added another, highly significant, sphere of reference to his work. He found that the Japanese interplay of nature and the garden site offered more design variations and combinations than any number of individual design ideas put together. This philosophy is very apparent in a site Haag has designed on Lake Whatcom, the Kukes garden, where he seems to have absorbed the natural elements and the surrounding landscape into his overall plan.

The Kukes garden achieves an unusual and beautiful liaison between the natural lake and the man-made summer cabin at its edge. The cabin is, in fact, a luxurious, though not ostentatious, home with panoramic views of the Olympic mountains. Acting like an echo of the lake, shore and mountains, are the blueish-grey, smooth natural stones that are piled up against the wooden chalet, creating surrealistic, Japanese-style scenery. Right down to the water's edge, Richard Haag has concentrated on simple hillocks, ending in three imposing, cement landing-stones which link the boathouse to the land.

Thirty metres above the lake, terraces for sitting out are positioned to give spectacular views. The pathways have been cleverly managed so as not to distract attention away from the stone theme. Cement grids, filled in with gravel of small stones (into which a few intrepid plants have found their way), are as unusual as they are practical. In the entire composition of the garden, Richard Haag has successfully shown his preoccupation with detail and harmony.

Opposite Richard Haag's highly individual use of loose stone creates an extraordinary rockery in front of the wooden chalet in the Kukes Garden on Lake Whatcom, USA.

Above right The cement grids used for the steps wind off down to the lake in a pathway that blends comfortably into the surrounding landscape.

Right Natural stones form an ornamental pyramid by the side of winding steps.

GARDEN IN A LANDSCAPE

◆

MASSACHUSETTS, USA

JANIS HALL

CREATING A GARDEN which relies for effect on the surrounding scenery could be considered one of the most difficult, but also one of the most inspiring, forms of design. The landscape of the garden must fulfil a number of disparate requirements, creating an interaction of indigenous and new design elements, whilst conforming to the demands of the site and to the client's aspirations.

The effect of scenery is not dependent on space or size. Some of the most beautiful scenery has been created in Japanese gardens where space is at a premium. For thousands of years, Zen masters have created garden scenery out of only a few hundred metres, miniaturizing mountains and raking dry rivers, grouping rock outcrops and simulating forests. American landscapers exploit as much space as is available, which is usually a great deal, yet the created scenery vistas are still a form of escape, a dream, to be composed with great artistry by the landscaper.

Janis Hall had a very eclectic education. She gained her masters in architecture at Harvard and then travelled and worked in both the East and the West. At an early stage in her career, she took classes with the great modern dancer, Martha Graham, whose vision incorporated ideas from Eastern thought, such as an identification with natural forces. Janis was also an apprentice to the famous Japanese sculptor, Isamu Noguchi, and tells of his great reverence for his materials. He used stone extensively, calling it 'a direct link to the heart of the matter'. He said that when he tapped stone with a tool, he would get an echo of what we are, and the whole universe would have resonance. This very broad experience of the work of artists in different mediums has given Janis Hall an innovative approach to design and scenery. In creating a landscape, she aims to follow her intuitive response to the materials and to the site, 'trying to work with the basic elements

Above A 'granite river', such as nature could have left thousands of years ago, has been manipulated by Janis Hall to convey the flow for her 'Murmuring River' at Great Hill.

Right The earth at Waterland is sculpted into wave-like forms that look as though they have been created by ancient glacial movement.

A view across the open landscape demonstrates how expansive the new landscape has become.

of our profession: air, earth, water and life (plants, people), in ways that engage our imaginations deeply.' In her numerous projects, Janis works directly *in situ*.

Waterland was formerly used as a gravel pit, later as a ten-acre residential site, and was in need of some restoration. Janis began the process by looking at the character of the surrounding countryside, where she found naturally dramatic, wave-like land forms, carved by ancient glacial movement. By removing all unnecessary elements (a rotting barn, paddocks, an old roadway, uninspiring dead trees and some unimportant broken stone walls), then sculpting the earth, Waterland became more visually powerful. Now the land is revealed as soft, nourishing and substantive.

The site provides a complex of experiences. If you are feeling strong and expansive, you can stride the ridge of a single berm from one end of the site to the other, all the while taking in sweeping views of the wider landscape, from one mountain range to another. Or, if you are feeling introspective and private, you can find refuge and tranquillity by walking along intimate valleys. The land now interacts with the other natural elements of the site in a meaningful way, creating a sense of mystery and the sublime – a peaceful power.

On the southern coast of Massachusetts, at Great Hill, Janis Hall has designed a landscape which totally harmonizes with its surroundings. Sculpture and landscape work together: wild flowers, wild grasses, local stone, sculpted earth, light and shadow, wind and water all interact. Her design involved cutting a sweeping, riverside edge between a meadow and a lawn, suggesting an image of the meadow as a riverbank and the lawn as a river. She massed plants in island-like configurations within the flowing meadow, creating a further ambiguity between water and earth.

The earth behind the house was sculpted in the form of a gentle, dry river bed, or wake, a visual echo of the bay of the sea which can be seen from the garden. The sea itself can be seen to heave and flow in shapes akin to those of the land, and Janis Hall has exploited this similarity of movement in her design. Light and shadow play both on the undulating earth of the garden and on the surface of the bay, as calm waters allow reflection and rough waters cast dark shadows. Janis calls her landscape Mnemonic River, a place where earth, air and water become barely distinguishable and dream, contemplation and experience become interchangeable.

Beyond the sweeping green lawns, a pond is planted with native wetland species, backed by a woodland of indigenous trees.

POSTSCRIPT

ENGLISH ROSES

A FTER THOUSANDS OF YEARS of inter-breeding in the wild, the rose has been subjected to centuries of cultivation and hybridization by man. Pre-eminent amongst the varieties now being produced are those of the group known as 'English Roses'. They are the achievement of former farmer David Austin, who has mixed eighteenth- and nineteenth-century roses with hybrid teas and floribundas developed in later years. There are now over two hundred varieties of English Rose available to gardeners around the world. The group's name was chosen because of England's special affinity with the rose.

Austin set out to create roses with flowers of old-fashioned cupped or rosette shape and a powerful fragrance. These virtues combine with a wide choice of colours, both delicate and rich, and excellent repeat-flowering properties of the hybrid teas and floribundas. The essential character of the old roses, as well as their more natural habit of growth, are also qualities captured in the newest English Roses. The early varieties had a tendency to be too 'top-bloom heavy' for their branches, but in the recent ones Austin has corrected this defect. English Roses will live on and flourish, their enduring charm providing a continuity between the old century and the new.

Above David Austin describes 'Constance Spry' as one of his most beautiful shrub roses, with its large, luminous pink blooms and its strong fragrance, similar to myrrh.

NEW RHODODENDRONS

A FEW YEARS AGO, I saw a mountainside in Switzerland covered in deep pink, low-growing rhododendrons. I was astonished, as I knew that the soil was not acid.

I thought then that one day a big breakthrough would allow the production of lime-tolerant rhododendrons. Little did I know that a German plant company was already hard at work developing such a sought-after species; and now they have succeeded.

I suppose that there are as many gardeners who hate rhododendrons as there are those who love them. The trouble arises if you happen to love them but garden on alkaline soil; to my distress, my own garden had been declared an azalea-free zone. But all this has changed with the arrival of new rhododendron varieties which will relax, thrive and produce splendid blooms in thick loam or clay, in soils with a pH between 5.5 and 7 and on exposed sites. My Swiss mountainside was devoid of any shade, yet the rhododendrons were flourishing.

Left The tall shrub rose 'William Morris', with flowers of formal rosette shape. It is extremely hardy and has excellent repeat-flowering and a strong fragrance.

A lime-tolerant rhododendron from the German Inkharo Project. Many hybrids have been produced including the *Rhododendron williamsianum* and *Rhododendron yakushimanum* large-flowering varieties.

Close on twenty years of research has informed the German Inkharo Project, working with more than 1.8 million seeds. The varieties produced come in a fine array of pastels and hot colours, from white, yellow, rose and red to blue, lilac and an attractive deep violet. The range is interesting, including hybrids with large flowers such as *Rhododendron yakushimanum* and *Rhododendron williamsianum*. If your soil is frost-free you can plant them at any time of the year, but they are hungrier than classic rhododendrons, so be sure to feed them well.

A bunch of genetically modified carnations. The cut-flower industry builds great hope on the diversity these techniques will generate.

GENETIC ENGINEERING IN THE FLOWER GARDEN

AS THE NEW CENTURY BEGINS, genetic engineering of new flower varieties is well underway. Biotechnology companies in Australia and Japan are already marketing genetically modified carnations, such as Florigen's dusty mauve 'Moondust' and 'Moonshadow' varieties, for the huge cut-flower market. It is also claimed that pest-resistant and repeat-flowering strains are readily achievable with genetic engineering techniques. It seems inevitable that this horticultural revolution will soon encroach on our gardens.

Most of the roses we cultivate today have been undergoing modification for hundreds of years. Yellow roses, for example, were hailed as a horticultural triumph around 1820. But do we really need to produce that elusive blue rose, the flower of legend? Would it be a gardening triumph or rather something to make us all a touch uneasy?

AUTHOR'S
ACKNOWLEDGEMENTS

It has been wonderful visiting many of the gardens shown in this book and where that has not been possible, I would like to thank the owners and designers who supplied me with photographs and information about their gardens. This brings me to thank the photographers, especially those who have let me use their photographs purely out of interest in the project. A book on gardens is a joint venture and every contribution is precious, which is why I would like to thank all those who have contributed. First of all my editor, Judy Spours, who has had patiently to cope with my 'Frenchiness'; David Fordham, the designer, on whose shoulders rests the look of the book, which is of prime importance; Jessica Puddy, who has had the task of turning my illegible text into computer language; Derek Kartun, my brother, on whom I have relied for some of the photography and much good critical advice; Lizzie Dymock, who has meticulously checked the ever-changing botanical names. And last, but not least, my publisher, Piers Burnett, without whom there wouldn't have been a book.

PHOTOGRAPHIC
ACKNOWLEDGEMENTS

Endpapers: Photonica. Page 1 & frontispiece: by courtesy of Charles Jencks. Title page: Martha Schwartz. Page 6: Andrew Lawson. Page 7: Didier Willery. Page 8: Caroline Tisdall. Page 9: by courtesy of Wifred & Jeanette Cass. Page 10: (left) Caroline Tisdall; (right) Claire de Virieu. Page 11: Otto Fried. Page 12: Didier Willery. Page 13: Caroline Tisdall. Conolt Park: pages 14-17, Caroline Tisdall. Ashton Wold: pages 18-20, Andrew Lawson. Vasterival: pages 21-26, Didier Willery. Chyyverton: pages 27-31, Derek Harris. All photographs of Charles Jencks' garden (pages 32-39) by courtesy of the owner. Pages 40 & 41: Andrew Lawson. Sticky Wicket: pages 42-46, Andrew Lawson. Hadspen House: page 41 & page 48 (centre), Andrew Lawson; pages 48 & 49 (top & bottom), Derek Kartun. The Caribbean: pages 50-55, Jim Scheiner. Cothay Manor: pages 56-59, Andrew Lawson. Page 60: Andrew Lawson. Page 61 and the LongHouse Foundation (pages 62-66): by courtesy of Jack Larsen. Majorelle: pages 67 and 70-71, Deidi von Schaewen; pages 68-69, Claire de Virieu. The Laskett: pages 72-75, Andrew Lawson; page 76, by courtesy of Jonathan Myles-Lea. Rio de Janeiro: pages 77 & 78, Kingsbury. Little Sparta: pages 79-83, Andrew Lawson. Page 84: Wirtz International. Page 85: La Bambouseraie. Arnhem: page 86 and page 90 (bottom) Piet Oudolf; pages 86-89, page 90 (top) & page 91, Andrew Lawson. New South Wales: pages 92 & 93, Leigh Clapp. Foggy Bottom: pages 94-96, Adrian Bloom. Manor Farmhouse: page 97, Michael Balston. Bambouseraie: pages 98-101, La Bambouseraie. Pages 102 & 103: Andrew Lawson. Abbaye d'Orsan: pages 104-107, Deidi von Schaewen. Mazes: pages 108 & 109, Adrian Fisher. Water Maze: page 110, by permission of Hever Castle. Urban Grottoes: Page 111-113 and 114 (left) by courtesy of the owner; page 114 (right) Marianne Majerus. Victoria, Australia: pages 115-117, by courtesy of Margot Knox. La Garde Adhemar: pages 118 & 119: by courtesy of La Garde Adhemar. Heligan: pages 120-122 and 125, Andrew Lawson; page 123 (top) David Hastilow; page 123 (bottom) Colin Howlett; page 124, Charles Francis. Page 126: by courtesy of Wilfred & Jeanette Cass. Page 127: Sally Matthews. Hat Hill Copse: pages 128-134, by courtesy of Wilfred & Jeanette Cass. Live Animals: pages 135-137, Sally Matthews. Ephemeral Forms: page 1387, Charles Francis; page 139, by courtesy of the designer. Il Giardino: pages 140 & 141, by courtesy of Daniel Spoerri. Page 142: Roger Foley. Page 143: Hugh Dargan Associates. Gent: page 144, Philippe Banduel. Washington D.C.: pages 145-149, Roger Foley. Bath: pages 150 & 151, Derek Kartun. Atlanta: pages 152 & 153, Hugh Dargan Associates. Dordogne: page 154, by courtesy of Kathryn Gustafsen. Munich: pages 155-157, Kingsbury. Page 158: by courtesy of Jose de Yturbe. Page 159: Martha Schwartz. Mexico City: pages 160-164, by courtesy of Jose de Yturbe. Boston: pages 165-167, Martha Schwartz; pages 168 & 169, Alan Ward. Pages 170 & 171, Andrew Lawson. Beth Chatto's Garden: pages 172-176, Andrew Lawson. Denmans: pages 178, 180 & 181, Andrew Lawson; other photographs by courtesy of John Brookes. Surrey: page 183, John Glover. Sunnymede: pages 184 & 185, by courtesy of Henry Clyne. Page 186: Wirtz International. Page 187: Robert Putzel. California: pages 188-190, by courtesy of the designer. Woburn: page 191, Derek Kartun. Quaker Hill: pages 192 & 193, Keir Davidson. Baruch: 194 & 195, Wirtz International. Page 196: Marc Keane. Page 197: by courtesy of Richard Haag. Zurich: pages 198 & 199, by courtesy of the designer. Corsica: pages 200-202, Paul Maurer. Kyoto: page 203 Haruo Hirota; pages 204 & 205, Marc Keane. Washington State: pages 206 & 207 by courtesy of Richard Haag. Massachusetts: pages 208 & 209, by courtesy of Janis Hall. Page 210 & 211: David Austin Roses. Page 212: (top) Derek Kartun; (bottom) by courtesy of the breeders.

INDEX OF PLANT NAMES

GENERAL INDEX